# About Island Press

Since 1984, the nonprofit organization Island Press has been stimulating, shaping, and communicating ideas that are essential for solving environmental problems worldwide. With more than 1,000 titles in print and some 30 new releases each year, we are the nation's leading publisher on environmental issues. We identify innovative thinkers and emerging trends in the environmental field. We work with world-renowned experts and authors to develop cross-disciplinary solutions to environmental challenges.

Island Press designs and executes educational campaigns, in conjunction with our authors, to communicate their critical messages in print, in person, and online using the latest technologies, innovative programs, and the media. Our goal is to reach targeted audiences—scientists, policy makers, environmental advocates, urban planners, the media, and concerned citizens—with information that can be used to create the framework for long-term ecological health and human well-being.

Island Press gratefully acknowledges major support from The Bobolink Foundation, Caldera Foundation, The Curtis and Edith Munson Foundation, The Forrest C. and Frances H. Lattner Foundation, The JPB Foundation, The Kresge Foundation, The Summit Charitable Foundation, Inc., and many other generous organizations and individuals.

The opinions expressed in this book are those of the author(s) and do not necessarily reflect the views of our supporters.

# Healing Grounds

# Healing Grounds

## Climate, Justice, and the Deep Roots of Regenerative Farming

Liz Carlisle

with Illustrations by Patricia Wakida

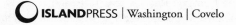

**ISLAND**PRESS | Washington | Covelo

Library of Congress Control Number: 2021945110

All Island Press books are printed on environmentally responsible materials.

Manufactured in the United States of America
10  9  8  7  6  5  4  3  2  1

*Keywords:* African American farmers; Asian farmers; Biodiversity; BIPOC farmers; Black farmers; Carbon sequestration; Farmers of color; Farmworkers; History of agriculture; Indigenous farmers; IPCC; Land access; Latinx farmers; Monocultures; Northeast Farmers of Color Land Trust; Organic farming; Racism at USDA; Regenerative farming; Soil fertility; Soil health; Structural racism; Sustainable agriculture; Sustainable food system; Traditional farming methods

Know the ways of the ones who take care of you, so that you may take care of them. Introduce yourself. Be accountable as the one who comes asking for life. Ask permission before taking. Abide by the answer. Never take the first. Never take the last. Take only what you need. Take only that which is given. Never take more than half. Leave some for others. Harvest in a way that minimizes harm. Use it respectfully. Never waste what you have taken. Share. Give thanks for what you have been given. Give a gift, in reciprocity for what you have taken. Sustain the ones who sustain you and the earth will last forever.

—Robin Wall Kimmerer, *Braiding Sweetgrass*

# Contents

# Foreword

As this book goes to press, the need for healing is on the mind of anyone who reflects on the times in which we live.

The world is falteringly emerging from a global pandemic that to date has claimed 3.8 million lives. Scientists from two US government agencies (the National Aeronautics and Space Administration and the National Oceanic and Atmospheric Administration) have just announced that our planet's "radiative energy imbalance"—the phenomenon underlying global warming—doubled from 2005 to 2019. Contrast that observation with the facts that our solar system came into being about 4.6 billion years ago, that we humans have existed on the planet for only the past 200,000 years, that the fossil fuel era began just 162 years ago, and yet within a span of 14 years we have doubled the amount of heat trapped by the atmosphere. This vastly outpaces anything observed in the planet's temperature record of the past 2,000 years. Headlines are documenting suffocating temperatures, droughts, dried-up rivers and lakes, raging wildfires, and violent storms, portending an era of climate instability, and an existential threat to humanity.

Add to this, we are contending the world over with the reverberations of a social order rooted in colonial conquest and extraction. Euphemistically called "racial reckoning," new movements demand redress of the rampant inequality created by global "development." Initially, at least, these overdue calls for justice are polarizing societies already strained by discordant worldviews about humanity's role in the biosphere.

There is need for healing, indeed.

It is therefore the right time for a sober and inspiring book such as this one. In the careful and competent rendering of Liz Carlisle, we see the way that these pathologies are related. And we also see a possibility that setting racial and social relationships right may lead to righting the planet's human-induced geophysical fever. Expressly, this work illustrates how human knowledge has already produced many pathways to meet the challenges of our time—if we but let this expertise flourish.

If this seems far-fetched, let me point to the book's extremely apt title. Liz could have chosen many other descriptively faithful options. (I'll posit as just three possibilities: "Agricultural Minority Report," "Untold Stories from the Food Underground," or "Global Agricultural Wisdom as Redemption.") But the brilliant two-word winner perfectly captures a theme running throughout this book: our salvation is literally underfoot, in soil—more properly, in how we interact with soil ecosystems that most of us don't see and therefore know little about, much less value. The double entendre of *Healing Grounds* is that there is a clear basis for the healing we need. But to survive, we must foment both the human and ecological diversity that have been suppressed by our history of homogenization, industrialization, and colonization.

Through spare, vivid storytelling, Liz illustrates the adaptive wisdom of Native American, African American, Mesoamerican, and Asian American traditions that may yet counteract the consumptive dead end of current agricultural practices. To be concrete, I'm referring here to methods that build soil fertility, store carbon, and produce abundant nourishment while providing good livelihoods—in spite of being countercultural in an economic milieu fixated on maximizing profits. In these pages, it becomes clear that suppression of peoples, their traditions, and their well-being has also suppressed other critical stores of capital: ecological and social. In an era that demands that we restore these vital resources, this is an extremely timely contribution.

Also welcome is Liz's temperate treatment of a complex history. (To give you an example of the flavor: "This is not to say there were no hierarchies or oppressive governance systems before White people showed up.") No idealized and unrealistic assessments here. Instead, be prepared to join the protagonists as they journey from worn and unexamined perspectives to rediscovery of time-tested principles. Just one instance is Liz's rejoinder to an axiom of the dominant economic order: that self-interest will produce the best outcomes for all. She shows instead the power of cooperative economics, what ethnographers have called *reciprocal exchange*, which is often dismissed as an antiquated feature of simpler societies. Reading these stories calls us to reexamine our assumptions both about these societies and our own economies.

One last note, before you proceed to the treasure that follows, pertains to the author. Professor Carlisle is an accomplished and multifaceted individual, as an intellectual, an academic, a writer, and an artist. In her earlier books, she figured as a key character, tying together her experiences with those of innovative farmers from her home state of Montana (and beyond). Here, she presents differently, and I wish to acknowledge that and to share the reason. As befits a book about how European suppression of global wisdom has led humanity astray, our author—a woman with proud European roots—has subsumed her role to that of an observer and humble learner. It isn't that she is a depersonalized narrator. In fact, she acknowledges that she had to examine and reformulate her initial premise for this book. But she deftly steps back, creating space for Indigenous, Black, Mesoamerican, Asian, and other persons of color in the foreground, to lead the narration. In fact, counter to a basic rule of writing—avoid repetition—Carlisle frequently, and honestly, repeats: "as I learned." It suits her well. And it will suit all who are privileged to trace her footsteps here on this journey of discovery. It is a journey profoundly relevant to our times, and which should fill you with hope in a moment when it seems there is a dearth of that essential human sustenance.

As a result of her careful effort, it is now your turn to learn.

**Ricardo J. Salvador**
*Director and Senior Scientist*
FOOD AND ENVIRONMENT PROGRAM
UNION OF CONCERNED SCIENTISTS
WASHINGTON, DC

# Can Soil Really Save Us?

In January 2021, Raphael Warnock became Georgia's first Black senator, gaining a seat formerly held by a Confederate general who allegedly led the Georgia branch of the Ku Klux Klan. A month later, he proposed a $5 billion fund for farmers of color, a step toward correcting, if not reversing, a long history of racism at the United States Department of Agriculture (USDA). The legislation, which eventually became part of a broader pandemic relief stimulus package, was covered in media outlets from the *New York Times* to *Modern Farmer*. Yet few reporters connected this debt relief to another headline-grabbing agricultural story that had been making the rounds six months earlier, back when odds of a Warnock victory still felt slim. That story was also one about righting wrongs—specifically, reversing decades of emissions by agribusiness. The world's preeminent group of climate scientists was suggesting that the answer to global warming might just be under our feet, in farm fields.

In early August 2019, journalists gained access to a leaked draft of a new special report crafted by the Intergovernmental Panel on Climate Change, or IPCC. The scientists argued that while a swift and sweeping global transition to renewable energy was necessary, it would be

1

too little too late. In order to keep warming below catastrophic levels, it would now be necessary not only to sharply curtail greenhouse gas emissions but to actually remove some of the previously emitted carbon from the atmosphere.

The report, which was eventually released on August 8, spurred widespread discussion of previously unfamiliar "negative emissions" technologies, whose enthusiasts basked in the sudden spotlight. One strategy that received significant attention was "bioenergy with carbon capture and sequestration," a geoengineering technology that involved burning plants or biowaste, then capturing the $CO_2$ and burying it. Another tactic, mineralization, proposed storing atmospheric $CO_2$ in carbon-rich minerals, including toxic waste from mines. A third approach, termed "direct air capture," used massive arrays of industrial fans to push air through a filter, where a solvent could be used to extract and capture the carbon dioxide. Since the biogeochemical flow of the process mimicked what might happen in a forest, the media took to calling these direct air capture plants "artificial trees."

Or, of course, you could use real trees.

The IPCC special report contained over three hundred mentions of "afforestation"—planting trees—and discussed several scenarios for slowing or halting deforestation. Significant emissions reductions and even negative emissions could be achieved in this way, the report's authors suggested. Planting trees and stopping clear-cuts of the Amazon rainforest had been central goals of the environmental movement for decades, so in a sense, this was nothing new. But what caught the attention of many journalists poring over the leaked draft was the way in which trees now figured in a larger discussion of the relationship between climate and the stuff trees grow in: soil.

As researchers have now known for decades, the majority of the carbon stored in forests around the world isn't sequestered in the trees, but in the soil below. Globally, soils constitute a carbon repository some three times as large as the amount of carbon stored in all the plants on Earth. This soil "carbon sink" is also three times larger than the amount of carbon currently in the atmosphere. And there's good reason to think that, with the help of plants, our soils could be holding even more carbon. A lot more.

The main reason soils aren't already holding more carbon is agriculture, or, more precisely, industrially farmed monocultures. Over thousands of years (and especially the last two hundred or so), carbon once stored in soils has been released to the atmosphere through overgrazing, plowing, and loss of soil fertility, as soils have been mined for their nutrients and left bare between plantings, prone to erosion. Researchers estimate that some 133 gigatons of carbon have been released as a result—approximately 8 percent of total global soil carbon stocks. The IPCC report and many of its readers started asking whether a different kind of agriculture might be able to repay the debt and put some of that carbon back.

In order to appreciate how carbon might be reinfused into soil, you first have to understand that soil is not an inert medium, but a diverse community teeming with life. Mediating the raucous nutrient exchanges belowground are billions upon billions of microbes, which can essentially digest carbon and store it beneath the soil surface. To do this, of course, they need a steady diet of carbon-rich materials—stuff like compost, mulch, crop residue, and, their favorite, plant roots. All this organic matter—microorganisms like bacteria, macroorganisms like earthworms, and the decaying life forms they like to eat—makes up the most ecologically significant portion of the soil.

Unlike geoengineering or direct air capture, sequestering carbon in the ground by adopting soil-friendly farming methods is relatively inexpensive and comes with multiple benefits. Carbon-rich lands are more fertile and hold more water, which improves resilience to droughts and floods. Practices that enhance soil carbon—like planting soil-building cover crops—also provide other "ecosystem services," suppressing weeds, reducing runoff, and providing habitat for pollinators and beneficial insects.

The prospect of a win-win solution for farmers and the planet rapidly attracted the attention of both media and industry onlookers, who began exuberantly promoting such practices as "regenerative" agriculture. The French government challenged nations around the world to commit to increasing soil carbon by four-tenths of a percent per year, based on a scientific analysis showing that such an effort could offset 20 to 35 percent of greenhouse gas emissions caused by human activity. In conservative states like South Dakota and Mississippi, no-till farmers and holistic management ranchers—who rotate their animals in ways that mimic native herbivores—began proudly calling themselves "carbon cowboys," spurring large-scale investments from General Mills and other major companies. The Rodale Institute, home to a forty-year-old experiment comparing organic and conventional agriculture, circulated a report claiming that more than 100 percent of current emissions could be offset through a global transition to regenerative organic farming. It seemed the world was poised to turn the carbon story of our food system on its head, transforming agriculture from a carbon source to a carbon sink.

But not everyone was convinced. The viability of the French initiative was widely questioned, as was the Rodale report. Concerns were raised that corporate carbon farming programs and agricultural carbon credit schemes might amount to little more than greenwashing. Scientists flooded academic journals with commentaries like "Managing for Soil Carbon Sequestration: Let's Get Realistic." The authors of this particular article pegged regenerative agriculture's carbon offset potential at no more than 5 percent—not even a quarter of the French team's *low-end* estimate.

But the real kicker came with a blog published by the World Resources Institute in May 2020, alongside the environmental think tank's new

*Creating a Sustainable Food Future* report. The blog, which immediately elicited detailed rebuttals from scientists and other regenerative agriculture advocates, was entitled "Regenerative Agriculture: Good for Soil Health but Limited Potential to Mitigate Climate Change."

I was no stranger to heated debates over the future of agriculture. I had, at this point, been researching the connection between agriculture and climate change for over a decade, and I was well-acquainted with the battle between organic farming proponents and those who argued that industrial agriculture was more efficient. In truth, I had already taken a side on this one. Both my reading of the evidence and my personal experiences in rural communities convinced me that well-managed organic farms were not only more efficient (expending far fewer resources to produce food) but also more environmentally sound. Yet this debate about regenerative agriculture and its carbon sequestration potential puzzled me, because even people in "my community"—the organic proponents—seemed to have widely divergent viewpoints. How could a climate solution that appeared so promising to one group of scientists be dismissed by another group of otherwise like-minded scientists as mere hype?

Hoping to have something more coherent to say about all of this to my ever-inquisitive students, I started asking friends who specialize in soil ecology for help. Was it true that regenerative organic farming methods could sequester carbon in the soil? How much? Would it stay there? After months of talking to colleagues, attending soil science conferences, and perusing journal articles with scintillating titles like "The Microbial Efficiency-Matrix Stabilization (MEMS) Framework Integrates Plant Litter Decomposition with Soil Organic Matter Stabilization," I came to an unexpected conclusion. Both groups of scientists were right.

As the critics warned, the somewhat simplistic approach to regenerative agriculture being aggressively promoted through carbon credit schemes was, for the most part, highly unlikely to alter the trajectory of climate change. For example, simply ditching the plow without making other changes might increase carbon levels near the soil surface but simultaneously decrease them at greater depth. Similarly, applying compost might just mean moving organic matter from one place to another—not actually building it up. But when I took a few steps away from Silicon Valley (where I had recently moved for a teaching job) and the investment community, I found deeper versions of regenerative agriculture under discussion, visions that were truly revolutionary. In these discussions, the math started to add up. Maybe we could actually make a dent in climate change if we tweaked more than just individual agricultural practices, if we reoriented the logic underpinning our entire food system.

I finally started to grasp the nuances of soil carbon sequestration in a conversation with Francesca Cotrufo, a soil ecologist at Colorado State University (and the author of the article on microbial efficiency-matrix stabilization). Soil organic carbon, Cotrufo explained, isn't all the same. At a minimum, we should understand this heterogenous substance as composed of two separate pools, or "fractions." Think of these two fractions, Cotrufo told me, like a checking account and a savings account, with plants making the deposits. One fraction is available for meeting day-to-day needs—after all, microbes need to eat too. The other fraction is stashed away in association with mineral compounds underground. Building up the savings account of soil carbon, Cotrufo stressed, involves a different set of processes than building up the checking account. Aboveground biomass—stuff like compost, mulch, and crop residue—is perfectly adequate for building up the checking account and creating fertility that farmers can immediately use. But if you want to build up a savings account too, you need roots. Carbon exuded by plant roots is nutritious and easy for microbes to digest. As a result, carbon from plant roots is five times more likely than aboveground carbon to be stabilized as organic matter in soil—the microbes gobble it right up and ultimately deposit much of it to their mineral-associated savings account.

So how does agriculture become more deeply (and continuously) rooted? Cotrufo had a few concrete suggestions. For one, farming systems ought to keep living roots in the ground all year long, by rotating diverse crops and using cover crops in the offseason. Perennial crops (like trees, alfalfa, or perennial grains) are a particularly elegant strategy, Cotrufo added, since they remain in the soil for multiple years and develop extensive root systems. In order to retain that stored carbon, plowing needs to be reduced or eliminated. And farmers might want to choose crops that allocate more of their energy to developing carbon belowground, rather than just pumping out the highest possible grain yields. But Cotrufo warned against oversimplifying this strategy, continually referring back to the forests and grasslands where she conducted most of her research before she started studying agriculture. Concerned by suggestions that fields be covered with monocultures of plants that store the most carbon, she cautioned that soil microbes don't respond well to such schemes. A healthy community of microbes needs a diverse diet, and if they can't get it from plants, they'll break open the soil carbon savings account to get at the nutrients inside, releasing stored carbon back into the atmosphere. For this reason, Cotrufo advocates mixtures of grasses (which produce a lot of carbon) and legumes (which produce a lot of nitrogen). "Basically, a healthy, diverse ecosystem," she said.

Speaking to Cotrufo left me wondering about the kind of agriculture she was promoting and whether it was being widely practiced—or if it had thrived in the past. Might there be a precedent for regenerative agriculture that could help people trying to create such farming systems now? I had an inkling of such a history, having studied the organic movement, but it was the kind of situation where I knew just enough to realize that there was a lot I didn't know.

I began conducting literature searches on the history of cover crops and the use of perennial plants in farming systems. Again, I called on colleagues, asking them for bread crumbs that might help me trace the origins of regenerative agriculture. To my amazement, I found that practices commonly promoted within regenerative circles as new innovations had been used for many hundreds and, in some cases, thousands of years—not just in far-away ancient civilizations but *continuously* and right here on the North American continent. Accompanying these practices were sophisticated analyses of soil health, as well as guidelines for stewarding it. Some of these regenerative farmers—though I came to understand them by other terms that they themselves used—were indigenous to these lands. Others had migrated here, bringing knowledge and seeds with them. But once I began learning to recognize the signature of their influence on the North American landscape, I started seeing it everywhere. Some of the most profoundly influential and knowledgeable land stewards in this country had no formal education in soil science, and many were not even counted as farmers by the USDA's Census of Agriculture. But in places that few of my fellow agricultural researchers ventured to look—vacant lots, immigrant neighborhoods, Native American reservations—regenerative agriculture kept periodically popping up, like a desert super bloom after a spring rain.

This left me with a pointed, haunting question. Why weren't these regenerative farmers more securely established? If putting down roots was the key to a climate-friendly food system, what was preventing these people with regenerative farming know-how from doing so? Or had they been uprooted?

What I eventually learned was neither simple nor comfortable, and it took time to sink in. It didn't hit me in a single revelatory epiphany, but one layer at a time, until my entire understanding of the food system had shifted. For years, I had been studying the dilemma of food as a relatively recent phenomenon, a conflict that arose in the wake of

World War II with the glut of chemicals and machinery. When corporations pushed wealthier farmers to use new industrial tools to grow large monocultures, small farmers were forced off the land and out of the market. In response, a coalition of rural communities and environmentalists fought back with the organic model, a more ecologically friendly way of farming that allowed farmers to get paid for the quality of their produce, rather than on quantity alone. As the decades wore on, the power struggle between "Big Ag" and small organic farms continued, each promoting their strategy as the best path to food security.

As I struggled alongside my fellow organic advocates, I began wondering if I'd failed to fully understand the problem. Had it really begun just a half century ago? And was it really just about the power of a handful of corporate meatpackers, chemical pushers, and grain dealers? I began looking further back in time. Before anybody referred to Iowa and Nebraska as farm states. Before Idaho became famous for its potatoes. Before Wyoming put a cowboy on its license plates. Before these lands were homesteaded, before the perfectly square sections could be seen from an airplane. When I no longer took these landscapes for granted, I could begin to see how they were created. And why they were doomed to fail from the very start. As I looked more carefully at the vast monocultures of corn and soy, I started to see not only the chemicals needed to produce them, the multimillion-dollar combines needed to harvest them, and the sprawling feedlots where they would eventually fatten confined animals. Increasingly, I also saw the full five-hundred-year effort required to create American agriculture as we now know it, an effort I would come to understand as one of the most significant events in history. And one of the most horrific.

It doesn't take a historian to recognize that the brutalization of Indigenous people was a fundamental part of US "settlement." But we tend to mentally separate that legacy from what is currently happening on the land. That disconnect allows us to denounce racial oppression while simultaneously supporting agricultural systems that were built on it. In fact, both human atrocities and environmental destruction stemmed from European societies' effort to remake the world in their image. The ships of military conquest sailed to the Americas on this idea, as did the ships of slave captains and settlers that followed. Indigenous people and their food systems were destroyed, replaced with European people and their plants. African people, themselves stewards of long-standing Indigenous food systems on their own continent, were kidnapped and enslaved, forced to grow agricultural commodities for White landowners. Waves of immigrants would face similar conditions—economically vital to a society that refused to admit them as full members. In this way, the American heartland had been broken. By the moldboard plows of settlers, yes, but simultaneously by the larger forces of which those plows were part and parcel—genocide, colonization, agriculture as domination. This story of climate and agriculture was, fundamentally, a story about racial violence.

As the aggregates in those prairie soils burst open, releasing hundreds of gigatons of stored carbon into the atmosphere, they bore witness to ruptures of life and limb, people and place, marking this violence in the biogeochemical record. The seeds of climate catastrophe were planted in this broken ground, I came to see, and only a full reckoning with that history could offer any hope of getting our planet back in balance.

~

At this point, I realized that I needed to examine the story of US agriculture—a story I thought I knew—through a lens other than my own. I needed to speak to people whose ancestors had experienced the slaughter of their bison herds, the enslavement of their entire family, the brutal exploitation of migratory farm work, or incarceration at the hands of their own government while their crops were left to rot. Aware that many people with such family histories were sitting right next to me at sustainable agriculture conferences, I became intensely curious about what farmers and communities of color might teach me about how to work toward healing on the land. When I asked the question this way, a rich landscape of regenerative agriculture began to come into view.

I spoke with Indigenous Montanans working to restore native prairie and bring home their bison relatives. I talked to "returning generation" Black farmers reaching back to their African heritage to inform new agroforestry initiatives. A Chicana soil ecologist—herself the child of farmworkers—showed me the results of her research with immigrant Mexican and Hmong farmers in California's Central Valley, whose highly diverse small farms were teeming with beneficial fungi. The more I learned, the more I came to see that regenerative agriculture was neither a relic nor a fantasy. It had always been here, but on the margins. Pushed to the edges of industrial agriculture, these practices had been sustained by people pushed to the edges of society. This was not just a story about regeneration but also one about liberation—and the two were powerfully intertwined.

In organic farming circles in my home state of Montana, I had been introduced to an agrarian philosophy descended from Thomas Jefferson, who famously waxed poetic about the virtues of those who worked the land. Small family farmers, Jefferson believed, were good stewards, good neighbors, and the ideal subjects to guide a democratic nation. "Those who labour in the earth are the chosen people of God," Jefferson wrote in his *Notes on the State of Virginia*, "whose breasts he has made his peculiar deposit for substantial and genuine virtue."

But what Jefferson could not quite bring himself to admit was that the majority of the people actually laboring in the earth of the nascent United States were enslaved. Following emancipation, the nation's agricultural labor would be passed on to slave descendants, then immigrants whose legal status was carefully manipulated to approximate a similarly oppressive social condition. Outnumbering by far the European American settlers whose homesteads became the rhetorical centerpiece of our

national agrarian mythology, these people of color were in direct relationship with the landscapes of this continent during the most transformative and consequential time in their history. Like the Indigenous
people who preceded them on the land, they knew all about soil getting
worn down and broken open. The story of the earth and its wounding
was their own story, their own wounding.

And yet, not everything was broken. As I learned from farmers,
scholars, and advocates who had spent lifetimes digging into these bur-
ied stories—some of them looking into their own families' pasts—the
regenerative farming traditions of their ancestors had been suppressed
but never fully snuffed out. Carefully tended in the gardens of the
enslaved and the murals of the landless, these traditions had provided
both material subsistence and another form of sustenance that was difficult to put into words. There had been centuries of this survival work.
Seeds braided into hair and smuggled across borders, passed down generation to generation. Bison and their human relatives, confined to
reserves, dreaming of reunion on their ancestral lands. *Milpas* on the
edges of farm fields. New Year's meals of black-eyed peas. Networks for
sharing harvest labor. All these practices had persisted, despite the con-
fines of structural racism. Might this moment of climate crisis be their
time to blossom?

∼

Nikiko Masumoto is optimistic. The third generation to farm her family's
certified organic orchard in California's Central Valley, the thirty-six-
year-old queer feminist performance artist–peach grower is well aware
that hers isn't the face that people typically imagine when they conjure
up an image of a farmer. But she is working to change that, to build an
agrarian culture that fully embraces diversity both on the land and in
the community. Part of that work involves situating herself in her own
family legacy on the land.

"Whenever I begin conversations about myself and my relationship to the land, it's always through my grandparents and great-grandparents who touched this same soil," Masumoto says. "There is a gift of that, which is thinking of my life in a lineage that is much more important than my own individual life." This sense of connecting across generations is central to regenerative agriculture, Masumoto believes. "So many of the methods that develop soil take time—the horizon is long. When you're wanting to leave a farm to several generations in the future you have a vested interest in taking up those practices."

But digging into her family's history is also a painful and complicated process. Discriminated against as immigrants, Masumoto's great-grandparents never owned the land they worked. What little savings they had built up was lost during Japanese American internment, when some 120,000 people—most of them US citizens—were incarcerated for years simply for the crime of their Japanese descent. So Masumoto's grandparents had to start from scratch, eking out a living on marginal land as they gradually built up the soil.

"We are the ones that the world needs in this climate crisis," Masumoto says, referring not just to Japanese Americans but to other communities of color who have experienced oppression. "Because we have those stories, we have that sense of fighting against the impossible."

As I continued my research, I heard Masumoto's sentiments echoed dozens of times. From Hawai'i to New York, Montana to Puerto Rico, young farmers and scientists of color were reviving ancestral regenerative farming traditions in a self-conscious effort to respond to climate change and racial injustice in tandem. These farmers and scientists understood regenerative agriculture not as a menu of discrete, isolated practices from which one could pick and choose and then tally up into a sustainability score. Rather, they saw regenerative agriculture as their ancestors had—as a way of life.

"For me agroforestry is not just about figuring out how to minimize your impact and still grow food within that system," says Olivia

Watkins, who is farming mushrooms in the understory of forested land in North Carolina that has been in her family for more than 130 years. "There are so many pieces involved in growing food that don't just have to do with the crop itself. The fungi in the soil. The wildlife in the area. How does water fall on the land? All those things are intertwined, so for me, the question is always, how can I be mindful of all those things?"

Watkins is equally mindful that she's conserving not only forest but also Black-owned land, which her family resolutely held on to over the course of a century when 98 percent of Black landowners were dispossessed. "With the history of oppression around land, the fact that we are stewarding the land and taking care of it is revolutionary," Watkins says.

On Watkins's and Masumoto's farms, what's being regenerated is not just soil but a complex web of relationships. As both women described to me, this form of regenerative agriculture can only be fully realized when the entire web is repaired so that the interconnected parts can function as a whole. This means attending to a component of the farm often left out of scientific discussions: people.

"I get pissed sometimes at ecologists," says University of California, Irvine researcher Aidee Guzman, "because they forget that people are involved in stewarding these systems." Guzman is herself an ecologist— she studies soil microbial activity and pollination on farms—but she's also the child of farmworkers who left their small farm in Mexico to immigrate to the US. When she looks at California's Central Valley, she sees thousands of people like her parents—people who have both the knowledge and the desire to steward regenerative farms, if only they had the opportunity. "We have to stop and think about the fact that farmworkers here in the US, people who were brought over from Africa and enslaved, they left *their* farms, probably extremely biodiverse farms," Guzman says.

Masumoto, who grew up just an hour away from Guzman, agrees. "Structured inequality in farmworker lives infringes on people's right to think about the future," Masumoto laments. "The very people who have the skills right now [to implement regenerative agriculture] are the very people who we have marginalized the most in this country."

In short, truly regenerating the web of relationships that support both our food system and our planet is going to take more than compost. We're going to have to question the very concept of *agriculture*, and the bundle of assumptions that travel with the English word *farm*. What is the objective of this activity? To convert plants into money? Or to foster the health of all beings?

We also need to think hard about who farms and why. Will agricultural labor continue to be structured as a punishment for the oppressed and a means of marking and fortifying class hierarchies? Or might it be woven into the fabric of social life for all of us, in ways that are regenerative for the human spirit and sustainable for the human body?

As we rethink farming, we'll likewise need to reconsider our relationship with land and whether we can or should own it. Decolonizing agriculture will require big changes in our economic system. But it will also require daily rituals, coming together for meals that connect us to the land and sustain our bodies as well as our ties to the sacred. "I think what we are learning, or perhaps relearning," says Masumoto, "is how to belong to a place. That philosophy is embedded in the practices you use to feed yourselves."

Building this kind of regenerative agriculture will require a much deeper understanding of what happened on these lands that we in the United States now call home. It's a complicated story and, in many ways, a painful one. But facing it squarely offers an irresistible promise: by coming together to rebuild these farmlands, we can not only heal our planet and its carbon cycle, we can heal ourselves and our communities too.

# CHAPTER 1
# Return of the Buffalo

Technically speaking, it was nearly summertime when Latrice Tatsey drove out to the Blackfeet Buffalo Ranch to dig the first soil pits for her graduate research. But having grown up on the Blackfeet Reservation—a dramatic convergence of mountains and prairie along the Canadian border in Northwest Montana—Tatsey knew she could encounter any kind of weather during June fieldwork. As the wind whipped up, she pulled a gray sweatshirt over her head, cinching the hood around her face to shield herself from both the chill and the soil, which kept gusting into her eyes.

Once she'd managed to dig a foot down into the chilly buffalo pasture, Tatsey stretched her body full length onto the earth, peering into the sink-sized hole. Here in the deep recesses of the soil, she hoped to find clues about how her people had lived in balance with this prairie for thousands of years—and how that balance might be restored.

Tatsey's path to bison ecology started when she was a young girl, growing up on a cattle ranch and going to rodeos with her dad. As a member of the Blackfeet Nation—or Amskapi Piikani, as Latrice's people call themselves—she was given the name *In-niisk-ka-mah-kii* (Buffalo

Stone Woman). "At first I was really upset," Tatsey recalls, "because I really loved horses and I wanted my name to have something to do with that."

But as Tatsey got older, she began learning the story of Buffalo Stone Woman. As elders shared with Tatsey, there had once been a very hard time, a starvation time, when the Blackfeet people couldn't find the buffalo and were running out of sustenance. One day, a woman went out to gather wood and came upon an iridescent, dark gray stone. When she picked it up, she was given a song to sing. The woman brought both the stone and the song back to her people, teaching others to sing with her. The next day, when they went out to hunt, they found the buffalo again. "When I first heard that story I was like, oh, wow," Tatsey recalls. "And I thought, maybe this isn't such a bad name after all."

Tatsey began dreaming of raising buffalo on her family's ranch, mentally superimposing the image of a herd onto the view out her window. "I would say, Grandma, you know where you see all your cattle?" Tatsey recalls. "One day I'm going to bring buffalo out here."

After finishing her undergraduate degree in natural resources, Tatsey landed a position with the agricultural extension service, administering US Department of Agriculture programs for the Blackfeet community. Her job gave her ample opportunities to visit the tribe's growing buffalo herd, which stoked her curiosity about the animals. Tatsey realized she had lots of questions about these native herbivores and their role on the landscape, but not nearly enough answers. So in 2017, she went back to school, this time for a graduate degree in environmental science at Montana State University. Which is how she found herself staring into a soil pit and trying to keep the dirt from blowing up her nose.

Only by looking underground, Tatsey told me, can you fully appreciate the key role that buffalo play on this carbon-rich but fragile prairie. By comparing soil samples from the tribal buffalo ranch and an adjacent cattle ranch, Tatsey hopes to document some of the interactions between buffalo and soils, which have important implications for the climate. But even on her first visit, she could already see potential signs of the buffalo that had been grazing this pasture for over twenty years. "There's more diversity in the plant species," Tatsey told me, "and the plant species are a lot larger in the buffalo pasture versus the cattle pasture."

We tend to think of grazing as a process of using up a finite resource, Tatsey explained, but for buffalo and most other native herbivores, it's more of a mutual relationship with plants. By selectively grazing over long distances, buffalo helped create one of the most ecologically productive landscapes in North America. Looking up from her soil pit, Tatsey can see for miles across this ancient prairie, 1.5 million acres of which still belong to the Blackfeet people—an area slightly larger than the state of Delaware. Rising up behind her, the Rocky Mountains create an "edge effect" on the Blackfeet Reservation, a zone of overlapping habitats that hosts some 80 percent of Montana's large vertebrates. "Our people call it the backbone of the world," Tatsey says.

To the many other species that call these prairies home, the buffalo's forage-boosting behavior means more food. But for humans in the twenty-first century, the impacts of buffalo grazing may have another important implication. "When you have healthier plant species," Tatsey says, "they are taking more $CO_2$ out of the atmosphere and bringing it back into the soil profile. Which potentially means buffalo could help us respond to climate change."

## Architects of the Prairie

Before Europeans arrived on the North American continent, some thirty million buffalo roamed its vast grasslands. (Scientists refer to the animals as bison, while most Indigenous plains people call them buffalo. "Sorry if I switch back and forth a lot," Tatsey explained in the middle of our interview). Ranging east from the Rocky Mountains, buffalo herds traveled nearly the entirety of what is now the United States, with the exception of Michigan, New England, Florida, and the Eastern Seaboard.

The historic range of the continent's largest mammal also covered a wide swath of Western Canada, all the way up to Alaska, and stretched southward into the northern part of what is now Mexico.

But buffalo didn't merely travel *across* these carbon-rich grasslands. They created them. Recently grazed areas generated nesting habitat for birds that needed bare ground, while areas the buffalo hadn't been to for a while were perfect for other species that required more cover. Since buffalo moved constantly, such patches of diverse habitat were scattered over the landscape, supporting butterflies, grasshoppers, and small mammals. Buffalo also rolled their thousand-pound bodies across the earth, rubbing off insects and shedding old fur. In the process, they formed depressions, or wallows, that filled up with water and became seasonal ponds. These wallows provided habitat too: researchers have identified several species of frogs and other amphibians that breed in them.

Buffalo formed a particularly intricate relationship with the plants they ate. As buffalo journeyed long distances, recently foraged vegetation had time to regrow before the animals came back. As the grasslands and the herbivores evolved together over many thousands of years, the grazing activity of the buffalo actually began to stimulate the plants in some cases, a phenomenon ecologists refer to as compensatory growth. Buffalo grazing also delayed some grasses from setting seed, keeping them in their growth phase for a longer period of time. It certainly didn't hurt that buffalo were leaving behind concentrated packets of fertilizer, which they reliably deposited out their backside everywhere they went. And as ecologists have recently learned, an enzyme in buffalo saliva helped stimulate plant growth as well. Along the way, the buffalo played referee among the prairie plants, grazing down the most dominant grasses to make space for less aggressive species like wildflowers.

By maintaining such a diverse mix of native plant species aboveground, buffalo were simultaneously shaping the ecosystem below the soil surface. To adapt to grazing pressure from the massive herbivores, prairie plants evolved to apportion a great deal of their efforts underground to support their extensive root systems. These root systems, in turn, delivered carbon into the soil, where it could be bound up in minerals and stored for eons. Over the millennia, buffalo helped build up the North American prairie into some of the most carbon-rich earth in the world. "The thing about native prairies," explains renowned soil scientist Asmeret Asefaw Berhe, "is not only that they store a lot of carbon, but they stabilize it underground for long periods of time, potentially hundreds or thousands of years."

Equally central to the intricate dynamics of these prairie ecosystems were the Indigenous people who lived in close relationship with the buffalo. "Bison were our wealth," Tatsey explains. "Bison were our economy. And how we managed them was our savings and what that meant is when the herds were healthy, our people were healthy."

Through careful observation, the Indigenous people of the Great Plains developed a sophisticated understanding of both the buffalo and the prairies, which allowed them to harvest abundant food, fiber, building materials, and tools without diminishing the population of the massive herbivores or disrupting the habitat on which they depended. "This Indigenous prairie food system was the longest-lived food system in North America," says Jill Falcon Mackin, a historian of Plains Ojibwe descent who is collaborating with buffalo restoration work at Blackfeet Nation. "It sustained us for thirteen thousand years at least; we believe longer than that."

Instead of confining the buffalo and attempting to turn them into livestock, the Amskapi Piikani and other Indigenous plains peoples followed the animals' movements, learning to anticipate their migration patterns. The people knew what time of year the buffalo would move to higher grounds, when hunting bands could harvest the animals by driving them off cliffs known as *pishkuns*, or buffalo jumps. They knew where the buffalo would go looking for tender young shoots in the "hungry season" of early spring, when most of the vegetation had yet to emerge from winter. And they even learned how to bring on these tender shoots a couple weeks earlier, by burning certain areas the previous summer or fall.

Learning from the animals' movements and employing selective burning practices, Indigenous plains people not only maintained the mosaic prairie structure created by the buffalo but significantly amplified it. "If the native foodways of the original prairie people in North America had not been interrupted in the way that they were by colonization," says agronomist Ricardo Salvador, director of the Union of Concerned Scientists' Food and Environment Program, "you really can't put much of a time boundary on how long those systems would have been viable. They had learned to be in equilibrium with an ecosystem that was grass based, that had herbivores in equilibrium with that grass-based ecosystem."

## Listening to the Land

When Europeans first arrived on the North American continent, they encountered many such food systems, fashioned over centuries by Indigenous communities managing a delicate balance with their unique ecosystem. On the East Coast, colonizers met the Haudenosaunee, whose practice of growing corn in mounds—often alongside beans and squash—sustained an impressive level of soil fertility for over four hundred years. When the governor of New France marched through Haudenosaunee villages on a mission of destruction and conquest in 1687, he could not help but be amazed by the productivity of the agriculture he found there. "The quantity of corn which we found in store in this place, and destroyed by fire is incredible," the governor wrote, boasting that he had demolished some 1.2 million bushels. The man's surprise is understandable, explains Jane Mt. Pleasant, a horticulture professor at Cornell University who has reconstructed and analyzed

Haudenosaunee farming systems. Haudenosaunee corn growers produced three to five times as much grain per acre as European wheat farmers in the same time period.

In the southwestern portion of what is now the United States, European colonizers found sophisticated societies living on mere inches of annual rainfall. Carefully harvesting what rain they received, and in some cases developing intricate irrigation systems, the Indigenous people of the arid Southwest successfully farmed the desert—without the devastating impacts of the massive water-moving systems that would remake the landscape in the twentieth century. Desert peoples learned to recognize and encourage a special class of plants, most of them succulents like cacti and agaves, which were uniquely evolved to dry conditions. While most plants rely on daytime sunlight to grow, these plants had the extraordinary capacity to harvest all the energy they needed at night, when they wouldn't lose too much water in the process. Their secret was a special photosynthetic pathway that became their namesake: the Crassulacean acid metabolism, or CAM. In the hottest, driest part of North America, Indigenous peoples built a significant portion of their food system around these CAM plants, which historically made up about a third of the plant species in their diet.

When colonizers eventually made it to Hawai'i, they found the Indigenous population managing interconnected ecosystems that ranged from forested mountaintops all the way down to the ocean. Through the ahupua'a system of land districts, Indigenous Hawaiians carefully conserved the upland forest, so as to ensure healthy watersheds and nutrient cycling for their crops below. With a human community whose numbers nearly matched the island's present-day population (which depends on imports for 90 percent of its diet), the Hawaiian archipelago was largely self-sufficient in food.

As the journals of explorers and even some military campaigners indicate, Europeans marveled at the abundance of food in the Indigenous

societies they encountered. The lush quality of the landscapes was frequently referenced as well, and some Europeans even observed that
Indigenous management was responsible for the health and productivity of these ecosystems. But to fully appreciate the genius of such
food systems would have meant acknowledging their architects' right-
ful claims to their ancestral lands, which the colonizers would not do.
Instead, they leaned into the doctrine of Manifest Destiny, which char-
acterized the North American continent as an unproductive and "sav-
age" wasteland, in need of the civilizing forces of European agriculture
and industry. Willfully ignoring regenerative food systems across the
Americas, Europeans proceeded to massacre both the people and the
creatures with whom they had lived interdependently for generations.

## Broken Ground

One of the most widely depicted elements of this genocide was the
slaughter of buffalo, which became a preoccupation for hunters and
the federal government alike. Photos and paintings from the nineteenth
century are rife with such images, depicting White men posed proudly
atop piles of buffalo skulls five times as tall as themselves.

Tribes fought back against the destruction of their food source, even
going without meat to conserve the buffalo that remained. Latrice's
father, Terry Tatsey, tells the story of Many Tail Feathers, a Piikani man
who was supposed to help with one of the last buffalo drives in the
late 1800s. The people had the buffalo gathered on high ground in a
pound, or corral, and were planning to run the animals off a cliff to
harvest their meat. But Many Tail Feathers had a dream that he had to
let them go, because their numbers were so small at that time. So he
released the buffalo, catching heat from a number of his fellow tribal
members who were concerned about the ever-worsening shortage of
food. "We were just going into that starvation era of our people," Tatsey
says, "but that was his responsibility from his spiritual helpers to sustain
those animals."

The efforts of Many Tail Feathers and others notwithstanding, however, nearly all thirty million buffalo were killed over the course of the nineteenth century, most of them in a particularly bloody twenty-year period. As land speculators and the US military understood, their strategy of exterminating most of these animals would profoundly undermine the way of life that had supported the people of the plains for thousands of years.

Less visible—to White observers anyway—were the other components of the prairie ecosystem that were simultaneously destroyed. Without buffalo and people tending the landscape, prairies lost the key drivers of their ecologically productive mosaic structure, which not only created habitat for grassland species but cultivated a diverse community of soil microbes belowground. Gradually, biodiversity on the prairie declined, slowly homogenizing the landscape as one niche after another disappeared.

Worse still, the majority of these prairies, once stolen, were redistributed to European immigrants, who were wholly unfamiliar with the arid grasslands of western North America. The settlers were instructed to plow up the "virgin" prairies, which rapidly released somewhere between one-third and one-half of their soil carbon to the atmosphere. During the twenty-eight years following the first European tillage, the productivity of the Great Plains decreased some 71 percent. A century later, much of the remainder of that soil carbon would be gone too.

In place of deep-rooted and diverse prairie vegetation, settlers were encouraged to plant large monocultural blocks of annual grains: shallow-rooted plants that could not survive on their own and had to be replanted each year. Unlike the Indigenous food system that preceded it, this agricultural method made no allowances for giving back to the land that supported the crops. Eventually, as settler agriculture drew down the land's fertility, farmers were instructed to use chemicals to supply nutrients to their plants. This did nothing to replace soil carbon and in fact added yet more carbon to the atmosphere, since fossil fuels were needed to manufacture the new fertilizers. Such fertilizers—far too concentrated for plants that evolved to take up slow and steady streams of biological nutrients—also turned into greenhouse gases themselves. Plants simply could not absorb all the ammonium nitrate, particularly given that monocultural farming systems didn't keep plant roots in the ground year-round anyway. Much of the chemical fertilizer either ran off into the watershed or migrated into the atmosphere as nitrous oxide, causing three hundred times as much warming, molecule for molecule, as carbon dioxide.

In places like Montana, where some land was clearly too hilly or dry to be productively farmed in this way, large areas remained grasslands. But while the changes wrought on the open range were not as immediate and violent as those that followed the plow, settler agriculture nonetheless gradually undermined the ecological balance of these untilled prairies too. In place of the buffalo that had evolved with these grasslands, European American ranchers imported cattle, which had been domesticated in ways that made human management easier but also necessary. To accommodate the needs of their cows, these ranchers began modifying the landscape. They manipulated water. They grew feed. But most consequentially, they built fences.

## Domestic Dependents

If there is one object that sums up the most insidious phase of settler colonialism, which picked up steam in the late 1800s and early 1900s, it is the fence. So steadily did barbed wire advance across the western United States, that just six years after the patent was granted, its inventor was already manufacturing enough to circle the world ten times. Of course, barbed wire wasn't meant to fence in the planet, but to corral cattle. Ostensibly, the barbed wire fencing was intended to protect cows from predators and prevent overgrazing, though the scientific basis of these claims has since been questioned. At the same time, it helped carve the West into discrete tracts of private property, where forage could be assessed, bought, and sold as a capital asset. With federal coordination and financing, thousands of miles of fences were built, turning Indigenous territory and open range into ranches. In a landscape where survival had long required mobility, life was now frozen in place.

Simultaneously, Indigenous people—those who had survived the military campaigns intended to kill them—were likewise rounded up and confined within the boundaries of reservations. The newly designated territories covered merely a tiny fraction of these peoples' ancestral homelands, often places that were habitable only in particular seasons. They were told it was for their own good, their own protection. That they would be more productive in settlement than migration.

To understand the origin of the climate crisis brought about by US grain agriculture, it's instructive to read the central piece of Federal Indian Law from this era, the 1887 General Allotment Act. Known as the Dawes Act, after the senator who proposed it, the law promised to carve up indigenous prairie ecosystems even further—not just into discrete reservations, but into discrete parcels assigned to individual tribal members. This was attractive to government officials because it allowed them to seize "excess" reservation land deemed "surplus." But it was also part of a systematic strategy to erase cooperative land management and remake Indigenous people as individual agricultural producers. As one proponent of the Dawes Act put it, "kill the Indian, save the man."

When many Indigenous people proved resistant to allotment, the federal government deepened their efforts at assimilation, sending Indigenous children off to brutal boarding schools. Separated from their families and forbidden to speak their language, they were forcibly trained in White cultural and agricultural practices, reinforced by a violent system of discipline that left many of the children dead.

In the early twentieth century, these attempts to "modernize" both the people and the landscapes of the American West were so tightly intertwined that "Indian affairs" and range management were often overseen by the same officials. They sought to homogenize and standardize, to make life legible so that it could be readily managed. They carved up interdependent communities into discrete individuals, erecting literal barriers between formerly connected lives. And in place of self-determining groups, they sought to create what Chief Justice John Marshall termed "domestic dependent" nations: populations that could not survive on their own, but must submit to hierarchical control.

## The End of Agriculture on the Prairie?

Such policies were not only genocidal, racist, and blatant violations of human rights—they were also wholly inconsistent with the ecology of grasslands. This became increasingly apparent as the twentieth century wore on and the failings of settler colonial agriculture became harder and harder to ignore. With the organic matter of these formerly carbon-rich prairies nearly spent, farmers had to apply more and more commercial fertilizer to produce a decent crop. Bad weather could be disastrous: the degraded soils of the West readily blew away in the event of a drought, as they did in dramatic fashion during the "dirty thirties" of the Dust Bowl. Similar scenarios played out on rangelands that had been overgrazed, despite abundant fencing. As both farmers and ranchers learned the hard way, soils with low organic matter dried out more quickly in droughts and waterlogged sooner with heavy rainfall. By the end of the millennium, such "extreme" events were occurring more frequently due to climate change, and farmers and scientists began asking how much longer agriculture could continue in the arid West.

In the face of such an existential crisis, it was on these prairies where the contemporary regenerative agriculture movement first blossomed, beginning in the 1980s. Desperate farmers facing the prospect of bankruptcy realized they had to do something different to avoid losing their farms. These farmers had come to distrust the agricultural industry, which sold them expensive inputs and lowballed them on grain prices. So instead, they began looking to one another for answers. Barnstorming folksy field days from Montana to Kansas, self-styled "carbon cowboys" began working to return soil carbon to their land. The most dedicated among them recognized that any successful food system in this part of the world would have to at least partially mimic the prairie. In place of monoculture, these farmers and ranchers diversified their crops, periodically seeding mixtures of plants for the sole purpose of feeding the soil, rather than harvesting everything. Some began focusing more heavily on long-lived perennial crops, recognizing their prevalence in the native prairie remnants that still survived on the edges of their farms.

But the signature practices of regenerative agriculture—the ones that would be most readily adopted and promoted—did not involve changing crops. Most of the carbon cowboys were pinning their hopes for healthy land on just two primary changes. For one, they reduced or eliminated plowing, to give soil microbial communities a chance to rebuild. And second, they adaptively moved their livestock to allow plant communities to recover, a practice that became known as regenerative grazing. Many of the Indigenous people I spoke to for this book expressed positive sentiments about this regenerative agriculture movement spreading across the plains, voicing hope that settler agriculture might be starting to learn how to better accommodate the rhythms of grasslands. But as both Indigenous and non-Indigenous scientists pointed out to me, these relatively minor modifications to "domestic dependent" agriculture were nowhere near enough to reestablish the balance of the prairie ecosystem and the carbon cycle. To accomplish that, they told me, we'd need to follow the lead of the regeneration already being undertaken by Indigenous people themselves.

## Bringing the Buffalo Back

When Latrice's father, Terry Tatsey, was a young boy growing up on a cattle ranch on the Blackfeet Reservation, he was fascinated by his grandparents' occasional reference to buffalo. "The stories weren't shared as much as I'd hoped they would be," Tatsey recalls, "because my grandparents at that time had experienced suppression of sharing information with us, and anything related to the old ways they wouldn't talk a whole lot about because of what they experienced by the federal government and the boarding schools." His grandparents' reticence only made Tatsey more curious, so he began reading anything he could find on the subject. "Any of the books I read on Blackfeet," he remembers, "there was always reference to our relationship and responsibility to buffalo."

In 1974, when Tatsey was a teenager, the tribal government began its first attempt to restore buffalo, obtaining a herd of animals from Yellowstone National Park. At that time, Tatsey explains, the tribe employed a "minimal management" philosophy, essentially allowing the buffalo to move wherever they wanted. As he watched the animals pass by his family ranch, Tatsey was amazed to see them establish a consistent pattern of movement—despite the fact that they hadn't been to these areas for generations. "They created a migration pattern that would come by my place in the springtime during the calving cycle and then up to the Rocky Mountains," Tatsey recalls. "Then in the fall time they would move back down and start their whole migration again."

Watching these buffalo reconstruct ancient memories of moving across the landscape filled Tatsey with awe and made him ever more curious about their history and behavior. But buffalo was almost a bad word at that time, he explained, since so many tribal members had been forced by assimilationist policies to earn their livelihoods as farmers or ranchers. Eking out a living on slim margins, the last thing they wanted was for a buffalo to trample their crops or eat up the forage they were counting on for their cows.

In 1993, Tatsey went to work for Blackfeet Community College, a tribally directed college offering a variety of two-year degrees and adult education courses. The lifelong rancher was hired to teach agriculture and natural resources classes, with an emphasis on outdoor experiential learning. He started looking for opportunities to get students involved in hands-on projects. Three years into Tatsey's tenure at the college, the tribal government decided to revitalize its buffalo herd and establish a new management program. In place of minimal management—which had a bad reputation with tribal farmers and ranchers—the tribe promised to control the herd's movements and keep them away from crops and cows. They gathered up the existing buffalo and sold off the vast majority of the animals, using the revenue to purchase a new herd that they hoped would be amenable to some rules.

The new tribal buffalo pasture became Tatsey's classroom. With the eye of a seasoned rancher and a background in veterinary research, he trained students to carefully observe the animals. Did they seem to be well fed and watered? Were they experiencing any health deficiencies? At the same time, Tatsey studied buffalo harvest methods used by Blackfeet people and created a presentation that he shared with each cohort of students. Fostering cultural connection alongside direct experience with buffalo, Tatsey believed, was key. "As the students better understood bison and their behavior," he recalls, "the acceptance by our people, even some of our tribal agricultural people, seemed to grow a little bit."

When the herd had been growing for about a decade, a group of Indigenous Canadians began planning a youth camp. Prior to colonization and the establishment of the border, these Canadian tribes and the Blackfeet had been part of one Indigenous nation, the *Niitsitapi*, or Blackfoot Confederacy. So the Canadian organizers of the youth camp asked a group from Blackfeet Community College to participate. A key part of the camp experience involved intergenerational conversations between young people and tribal elders, which stretched out over a series of days. As the conversations proceeded, a theme emerged: the need to more fully reestablish the buffalo. "It was that camp," says Tatsey, "that really started the whole effort for the Iinnii Initiative."

Previous efforts to restore buffalo had been undertaken by individual tribes, within reservation boundaries established by the US and Canada. But the Iinnii Initiative—named after the Niitsitapi word for buffalo—proposed a broader vision. All the members of the Blackfoot Confederacy would work together to collectively reestablish a population of animals that would once again roam freely across imposed borders. Tatsey, who was one of the founders of the initiative, helped to organize its first stage: a two-year series of elder dialogue meetings. "It was just learning and listening," he recalls. "We got the elders together to tell stories and share with us why it was important to bring the buffalo back."

Facilitating these dialogues was Leroy Little Bear, a lawyer and professor from Kainai First Nation in Alberta, who had helped found the first Native American Studies department in Canada. Little Bear, fluent in his native language despite the best efforts of his boarding school instructors, listened closely to the elders, careful not to cut off their insights too quickly. For hours, he simply paid attention, taking everything in.

After two years, Little Bear finally addressed the group, having gleaned two messages from the elders' stories. The first, Tatsey recalls, was a statement. "He voiced it almost as a statement from the buffalo: I never left you, you left me," Tatsey recalls. "Meaning we went to another way of life, the Western lifestyle." Following this statement, Little Bear placed an empty chair in the room and asked a question. "He said this is the buffalo sitting in the chair, this is the buffalo's question to all of you in the room," Tatsey remembers. "If I come back to you, the Blackfoot people, what will you do to help me, what will you do to protect me?" Little Bear went around the room, asking each of the Iinnii Initiative founders to answer the buffalo's question. How would they reintroduce the buffalo as a free wild animal? How would they work with agricultural producers to accept it? How would they work with other tribes and government agencies, across borders? "That made us think a little deeper," Tatsey remembers. "If we're going to really do this, what's our commitment to make sure this actually happens."

Tatsey came to the insight that a powerful way to secure that commitment would be through a treaty. But not the sort that his people had been asked to sign for the past couple hundred years. "If you look at our treaties with the US government," Tatsey explains, "it wasn't a good track record for tribes." In the second half of the 1800s, Tatsey told me, the Blackfeet were asked to sign several treaties, each taking away land and rights promised in the previous treaties, until the tribe had been dispossessed of most of their lands. "When our last agreement happened in 1895/1896," Tatsey says, "we ceded Glacier Park and we ceded the Badger-Two Medicine [an adjacent area]. Our people had to sign on as witnesses to that treaty."

Instead of signing on as witnesses to a treaty cooked up by White people, Tatsey proposed, how about crafting a buffalo treaty of, by, and for Indigenous people—with US government officials as the witnesses. "We agreed to have a treaty signing on September 23, 2014," Tatsey recalls. "I'll never forget the date, because it was my daughter's birthday. We talked with the superintendent of Glacier National Park. We talked with the superintendent of Waterton National Peace Park. We asked if they would be witnesses to this tribal treaty. And they agreed to do it."

Eight tribal nations within the Blackfoot Confederacy signed on to the Medicine Line Northern Tribes Buffalo Treaty on that day in September, pledging their commitment to the Iinnii Initiative. A dozen more tribes would sign on over the next four years, building momentum for the vision of a free-roaming, transboundary herd. Of course, somebody had to supply the actual animals, a job that fell to the buffalo managers at Blackfeet Nation. The problem was, they still didn't have enough space to build up the herd.

"When that herd we introduced in the 1990s grew to almost four hundred animals, we were getting pressure from locals that had concerns over them," Tatsey recalls. "So the tribal council sold off all but about one hundred animals." Tatsey and others worked to identify more land for the buffalo, a challenge in the wake of allotment policy. The legacy of the Dawes Act was a checkerboard pattern of land ownership, fractionated between individual tribal members, tribal governments, and non-Native ranchers who had purchased or leased grazing land. In this environment, putting together sufficiently large tracts of land to host buffalo was all but impossible. Nonetheless, Tatsey and his colleagues managed to scrape together a more sizable area—but it was divided between two separate ranges, some thirty miles apart from each other. The next challenge was getting permission from tribal ranchers to trail the herd across their lands twice a year, when the buffalo would make the journey between their winter and summer ranges.

Once the permissions were secured, the biannual buffalo drive became something of a hit, spurring a PBS documentary and considerable goodwill from both Native and non-Native observers. Tribal members astride horses and four-wheelers herded the animals, while others in pickups held up traffic to allow the buffalo to safely cross busy roads. "For this certain time of bringing these animals back and forth to the winter and summer ranges, it brings people together and creates that community togetherness," remarked Blackfeet Buffalo Program director Ervin Carlson in the 2016 documentary about the drive. "These animals created that."

But as Carlson and Tatsey both knew, the animals being driven between winter and summer ranges were semidomesticated. This was the status of most buffalo available for purchase, some five hundred thousand of which were being raised for meat production in the US and Canada and managed like cattle. By contrast, just thirty thousand buffalo were in conservation herds, only half of those in tribal hands, and virtually none with space enough to resume their historical patterns of movement. And yet, the Iinnii Initiative called for a wild herd, animals that could migrate on their own. So Tatsey and his colleagues started looking for animals that might have descended from the original wild herds on the northern plains, buffalo that hadn't been seen in this place for over a hundred years.

They found such buffalo in an unexpected place, just north of the Canadian border on the Elk Island Reserve in Alberta. Before moving to Alberta, this herd had spent decades on the Flathead Indian Reservation in Pablo, Montana, which was typically referenced as their point of origin. But meticulous research revealed an earlier chapter in these buffalo's story: back in the 1870s, this herd had roamed wild at Blackfeet. In 2016, eighty-eight of them came back home, where the Blackfeet Buffalo Program began preparing them for a life of freely traversing their full historical range.

The area where the tribe plans to release the buffalo—just south of the Canadian border, near the sacred site of Chief Mountain—is already tribal territory, part of the present-day Blackfeet Reservation. But if reintroduction is successful, and the buffalo resume their historical migration pattern, they won't stop at the reservation boundary. Instead, tribal buffalo managers and their collaborators believe, the animals will migrate into adjacent jurisdictions: the Lewis and Clark National Forest, Glacier National Park, and even across the border into Waterton Lakes National Park in Canada. When the Iinnii Initiative first approached the agencies about this possibility, Tatsey says, it wasn't clear what would happen. "We asked them, what happens if they migrate into these areas that are part of our ceded properties anyway, where we still have reserved rights," Tatsey recalls. "At first, they wouldn't say nothing. Then, it was like, if you guys *push* them back in there, you trigger NEPA [National Environmental Protection Act] and all these other regulations, but if they *migrate* there and you can't get them back out . . . that's different."

As talks went on, agencies began to openly embrace the possibility of hosting the buffalo, fostering just the sort of tribally led, government-to-government dialogue Tatsey had hoped to create with the 2014 treaty. "There will be transformation of landscape in Glacier National Park, but we believe that it will be a transformation that will take it back to what it was like when there were natural free ranging bison on the landscape," the park's superintendent Jeff Mow told a reporter in 2018. "Instead of sitting across the table with the Tribe, we're actually sitting around the table thinking about how we're going to manage this wildlife in a shared area for this shared vision."

## Buffalo in Cattle Country

As Tatsey and his collaborators move forward with their plans for wild buffalo, however, they remain well aware of the concerns of tribal ranchers. As a rancher himself, Tatsey is sympathetic to these worries. "I get more calls from my friends and fellow ranchers," Tatsey told me. "And they say, if we allow these animals into our range units that we have for livestock, they're going to take the grass we paid for." The tribe leases parcels of grazing land (known as range units), to individual ranchers, Tatsey explained. These lessees naturally feel entitled to benefit from their investment by fattening their own animals—not wild buffalo. In certain cases, the tribe has been able to arrange land swaps, moving impacted ranchers to range units outside of the area proposed for free-ranging buffalo. But not all the land is owned by the tribe: some was actually sold off to individual "allottees" during the Dawes Act era. "This is not easy," Tatsey acknowledged. "Even the land that the tribe owns, if the bison are grazing it and it's not part of the range unit system anymore, the tribe would lose the revenue that they raise from leasing that land out to individuals. So that's going to be an economic challenge for us."

Taking this economic challenge head on, the tribe took an unprecedented step in 2019, creating its own Agricultural Resource Management Plan. The plan, which identifies available agricultural resources and establishes management objectives directed by the tribe, is the first such effort undertaken by a US Indigenous community, and its implementation has been funded by a $2 million grant from the Foundation for Food and Agriculture Research.

The Iinnii Initiative buffalo reintroduction project is the first item on the plan, which also spells out a strategy for establishing a Blackfeet national park on tribally controlled lands adjacent to Glacier. Alongside cultural benefits, the plan lists economic opportunities that could come with such a park: gate entrance fees, toll roads, and tourism services like campgrounds and guides. Yet the plan also proposes another land conservation initiative, focused not on creating more wild areas but on preserving healthy forage on ranches. This proposed prairie land designation would focus on sustaining healthy grasslands for grazing—by either buffalo or cattle.

But what's really gotten ranchers' attention is the plan's proposal to build a new multispecies processing facility: a culturally appropriate slaughterhouse that could process both beef and buffalo, right on the reservation. For tribal ranchers who have always had to market their cows off the reservation—accepting the low prices and abysmal conditions that prevail in the meatpacking industry—this could be a game changer. The plan spells out a process for creating a Blackfoot Prime agricultural cooperative and a label to be shared across the Blackfoot Confederacy, which would allow tribal ranchers to reach environmentally and socially conscious consumers who are willing to pay a premium for humanely and sustainably raised meat. The tribe is currently studying these economic impacts, which could substantially improve the livelihoods of tribal livestock producers and the community as a whole. The facility would also make such meat available locally, which could have significant public health benefits.

"Pound for pound, bison meat has much higher protein and much lower fat than beef," says Mariah Gladstone, a Blackfeet educator and entrepreneur and founder of the online cooking show *Indigikitchen*. The two meats, Gladstone says, also have a different balance of omega fatty acids. Grain-fed beef has comparatively more omega-6s, fatty acids that are overly emphasized in the Western diet, driving inflammation and risk of chronic disease. Buffalo meat is richer in omega-3s, which actually fight inflammation—while improving heart health, mental health, bone density, and infant brain development.

"If people were to consume bison for all the beef they are consuming, I think we'd see radically different health outcomes," Gladstone says, explaining that it's not just a matter of individual nutrients. "Partly, it's because of your basic fat and protein, fewer saturated fats, more omega-3s. But also, on a broader scale, to be able to recognize the foods that come from the land and the connection that those foods have to the inherent value of our identities and our landscapes . . . I think when you know where your food comes from, when you see your food grow-ing up every day, you are more passionate about doing the work that it takes to ensure that those spaces that you rely on for food are taken care of. You're less likely to support projects that might poison the water that those bison rely on."

But even as Gladstone and others I spoke to at Blackfeet compared buffalo and cattle, they described them less as adversaries and more like teacher and student. Cows have a better nutritional profile, Gladstone says, when they forage their own diet—as buffalo historically have done. They are also easier on the landscape when people move them more often, another lesson from the buffalo. "I think there would be a benefit of having bison and looking at the behaviors that are healthy for the landscape," Terry Tatsey says. "Those are things that hopefully we as livestock producers can emulate." His daughter Latrice agrees. "I know the big thing within ranching is this term they're using, regenerative grazing, where you only hit a specific field for a certain amount of time with a certain amount of animal numbers and then you don't utilize it for a specific period of time," she says. "For me that's pretty much mimicking how bison naturally already utilize the land."

As a proponent of buffalo restoration who also depends economically on her family's cattle ranch, the younger Tatsey is in a unique position to reach out to fellow tribal ranchers who remain skeptical. She's convinced more than one rancher to change their minds about buffalo, her dad said. But it hasn't been easy. "She had to work a year and a half just to identify tribal producers that were willing to work with her on her research," Terry said of his daughter. "They thought this might be something punitive for them for overgrazing or not using proper grazing practices."

Latrice attended several workshops with livestock producers, explaining that she wasn't grading anybody's performance and that no one was taking away their range units. The goal was to compare cattle grazing with buffalo grazing, to see if the native herbivores might have some benefit to the land. If so, she explained, they could potentially point the way to more profitable cattle management—or the ranchers might eventually consider switching to buffalo themselves, as she'd been dreaming about since her childhood conversations with her grandmother. Her patient outreach work paid off, says Terry. "Now she has tribal producers contacting her, asking if she could do soil analysis of their land."

### Ancient Animals for a New Climate?

Research is critical, Latrice Tatsey explains, because it's helping her answer the question posed by her elders: if buffalo come back to the Blackfeet people, what will the people do for the buffalo? On the one hand, Tatsey and other researchers are exploring the "human dimensions" of this question, working with ranchers to craft a nuanced approach to buffalo restoration that won't trigger the backlash of the past. But keeping their promise to the buffalo also requires tackling ecological riddles, many of which are challenging to definitively solve. It's been more than a hundred years since buffalo last completed their historic migration cycles on these grasslands, and both the vegetation and the climate have undergone significant shifts in their absence. After thousands of years of buffalo providing the link between people and the land, the roles have reversed, with people now needed to bridge buffalo back into relationship with the prairie. This is why Tatsey chose to study soil ecology: it's a way to support buffalo in rebuilding the landscapes that will ultimately support us all.

As a graduate student in land resources and environmental sciences at Montana State University in Bozeman, Tatsey joined forces with a number of researchers asking similar questions. Partnering with the buffalo restoration program at Blackfeet, Tatsey and her colleagues are documenting the animals' interactions with the prairie ecosystem and trying to anticipate how these might shift with the warming climate. How do buffalo affect the biodiversity of the landscape? How do they impact soil carbon? How do they do in extreme weather events?

Bruce Maxwell, one of the professors in Tatsey's graduate program, started thinking about these questions one day while he was headed out for a hike. On the way to the trailhead, he passed a property owned by Ted Turner, where cattle had been replaced with buffalo and most of the internal fences had been ripped out in an attempt to restore the riparian areas. Maxwell peered into the pasture, trying to figure out whether the project was working. "At that point these were just casual observations from driving through to the trailhead to Spanish Creek," he said.

But as Maxwell started thinking more about climate change—and the implications for Montana agriculture—he began systematically researching buffalo restoration. To meet food demand under climate stress, Maxwell reasoned, the US may need to convert its most productive lands—midwestern farms that currently grow corn and soy to feed cattle in feedlots—to direct food production for people. This would mean raising our meat entirely on grass, in places like Montana. "Then, I start thinking, is that even wise because beef is not doing well in these increasingly hot summers," Maxwell says, "and the direction in beef genetics has been moving toward black cows, and they do worse than any when it is hot. So that led me to think, is there a better breed, and then gee, there's a better animal!"

Buffalo fare better under hot and dry conditions than cows, Maxwell learned—both from reading research papers and from talking to ranchers who've worked with both species. "If we start to get hot enough that it's really difficult to grow grains and even some of our rotational crops," Maxwell says, "rather than producing more corn for ethanol and cow feed, we ought to be thinking about how do we best adjust. If we can finish bison in Montana on grass or locally grown crops and process them in small facilities scattered around the state, probably on reservations, this could be a win-win situation."

Convinced that buffalo could be the future of Montana agriculture, Maxwell set up a research collaboration with Blackfeet Nation and Blackfeet Community College. As he began learning from tribal bison managers, three things were apparent almost immediately: predators didn't bother the buffalo, the herd did just fine with extreme weather, and they moved almost constantly. For Maxwell, who grew up in Montana and has spent a lifetime hearing about conflicts between ranchers and wildlife, the buffalo's response to predators was particularly noteworthy. The area where the Blackfeet are planning to restore a free-roaming herd isn't the kind of place you'd leave cows on their own, he explained, or at least not without a lot of worrying. Hundreds of grizzly bears roam the areas in and around Glacier Park, as do packs of wolves, who've been successfully reintroduced in recent years to the chagrin of some cattle producers. "On one bison ranch in this area, they observed thirteen grizzly bears last May," Maxwell says. "They have wolves too, but none of that seems to bother the bison much."

And then there was the matter of extreme weather. In Montana, climate change not only means hotter, drier summers but also more severe winter storms. How would grazing animals deal with huge drifts of snow? A historic September cold spell answered Maxwell's question. "There were fifty-two inches of snow in Babb (a small town within Blackfeet tribal lands) and the bison didn't care." Maxwell said. "A lot of cows died in that region, even adult cows. This just demonstrates that these animals are so much better suited to our system and probably best suited to the future kind of conditions that we might be encountering."

One of the main reasons buffalo are so well adapted to the northern prairie, Maxwell explained, is that they move so much. "Ranchers do all this work to rotate cows under modern management practices," Maxwell says. "Bison, they do their own rotation." Maxwell described a conversation with a ranch manager, who estimated that cattle spend about 80–90 percent of their time with their head down, feeding. "With bison, they feed only about 30 percent of the time, and the rest of the time they are socializing—or that's what he called it," Maxwell recalls. "We were sitting there watching a bison herd while he was telling us this story, and it was remarkable how little time they were feeding and how much time they were kind of interacting in funny, different ways."

Latrice Tatsey is fascinated by buffalo's patterns of moving and grazing, which are so different from the cattle she's been observing and caring for her whole life. "A lot of times they'll pick certain plant species that are more dominant than other plant species," Tatsey observes. "What I see buffalo doing is returning a natural balance." One of the hypotheses Tatsey is keen to explore is that buffalo grazing behavior might be driven by chemicals released by plants, known as volatiles. "If buffalo have evolved on these landscapes from time immemorial, is there a way that these plants send out specific volatiles that attract the bison species?" Tatsey wondered aloud during our interview, suggesting this might be the focus of her next research effort. "I want to know, is there a specific thing the plants are releasing, like 'Hey, we're ready, come eat us.' Or 'Hey, we're not ready.' Are there cues that keep them from eating a specific plant at a specific time period?"

## A Mosaic on the Prairie

As the Blackfeet work toward a free-roaming herd, Tatsey and other researchers try to predict how the animals will respond to life without fences by looking to a small handful of large buffalo populations in Montana, Kansas, and Oklahoma. Established by conservation groups, often with university partners, these restoration experiments are the only places where buffalo currently have enough space to move as they wish.

The newest of these experiments, the American Prairie Reserve, is just 150 miles east of the Blackfeet Reservation. By buying out ranchers and purchasing leases to graze federal land, the reserve's founders are attempting to build up the largest restored prairie in the United States, hoping to eventually put together an area the size of Connecticut. They've already acquired a significant share of the land and released hundreds of buffalo, which are carefully tracked and monitored as they graze. The project is controversial, mainly because it's backed by ultra-rich Silicon Valley investors who didn't consult locals before starting to aggressively pursue buyouts. Nonetheless, the science conducted there has generated useful data—the reserve has already documented faster growth of riparian vegetation on its buffalo pastures, which provide corridors for other grassland species.

But for longer-term studies of buffalo grazing, Tatsey and her colleagues have to look south, where the Nature Conservancy has been preserving prairie and restoring buffalo for several decades. Beginning with the 8,600-acre Konza Prairie Biological Station near Manhattan, Kansas, which the conservancy cofounded with Kansas State University in

1971, the nonprofit went on to establish an even larger reserve in 1989, near Pawhuska, Oklahoma. The Tallgrass Prairie Preserve stretches across nearly 40,000 acres, more than half of which are populated with some 2,500 free-ranging buffalo. With this much space, the preserve has been able to reestablish one of the key historic management practices used by Indigenous people on the Great Plains: burning. "What we've found is that fire and grazing interact, and that's actually what creates the biodiversity that occurs on grassland," says Sam Fuhlendorf, a professor of rangeland conservation at Oklahoma State University who has been collaborating with the preserve for some two decades. "This isn't a new idea, this is what Indigenous people did before Europeans got here."

Buffalo preferentially graze recently burned patches, Fuhlendorf explains, where the forage quality of the fresh, tender plant life is about four times higher. Other patches don't get grazed for years, until they build up enough fuel and eventually burn as well, attracting the buffalo back. With different pieces of the prairie all in different parts of this cycle, the landscape becomes a constantly shifting and uneven mix of thick brush, bare ground, and everything in between. Birds love it, Fuhlendorf says.

"When prairie chickens nest," Fuhlendorf told me, "they're looking for the thickest grass they can get into. They need grass that's not burned or grazed for nesting habitat. But when they get their broods, that vegetation is too thick, they need something that's real patchy, so the chicks can move through it and get insects." Lesser prairie chickens are dwindling in numbers, Fuhlendorf explained, as are a number of other grassland bird species that ecologists are concerned about. He's frequently asked how to create the best possible habitat for these threatened species, but there's no one right answer, he says.

"In the western Great Plains, there's a mountain plover that's endangered," Fuhlendorf says. "It will nest sometimes on farm fields that are plowed that have nothing growing, prairie dog towns that have nothing growing, or recently burned areas where animals are heavily grazing. But if you pick a different species, it requires the exact opposite and they live in the same area."

The native birds' diametrically opposed habitat requirements frustrated Fuhlendorf early in his career, making conservation seem like an impossible task. "I read this one paper from the seventies," he recalled. "They had variables like grass height, and one bird population would go up and one would go down. So you're like, well, I guess you can't have those two birds."

Fuhlendorf eventually realized that it wasn't a matter of picking winners and losers: you simply had to have lots of different types of habitat available in any given area. This was exactly what buffalo created, particularly in the presence of fire—or another form of disturbance, such as multiple species grazing the same prairie. "The herbivore populations on this landscape were really diverse historically," Fuhlendorf says, "and it wasn't just all bison; there were pronghorn, and there were elk and lots of other herbivores, prairie dogs. If you restored all those species, probably you could get similar dynamics as with fire."

John Briggs, who served as director of the Konza Prairie Biological Station for more than a decade, came to the same conclusion. "If the Nature Conservancy asks you for money to preserve tallgrass prairie," said Briggs, who had clearly heard hundreds of such pitches over the course of his career, "they show you this nice flowing sea of grass, six to eight feet. I've seen it like that a couple times in my life: you can literally go in the grassland and get lost because the grass is so tall." But such scenes are actually quite rare on a grazed prairie, Briggs told me, and not necessarily desirable. "Without grazers, a few grass species become dominant," Briggs said. "You might get ten or twelve species of plants per square meter. You introduce grazers, that plant diversity jumps up to twenty to thirty species per square meter."

Returning to what was now becoming a familiar refrain in my conversations with researchers, Fuhlendorf noted that such plant diversity also has implications for the soil. More legumes in the mix mean more nitrogen below the surface, which has untold cascading impacts on the diversity and productivity of the soil microbial community, and thus the forage. I later learned that Fuhlendorf had even applied his heterogeneity theory to his own lawn—for a few hours. "I have three acres in the town of Stillwater," he told me, "and I would get really tired of mowing it. One day, I decided to raise and lower the mower randomly, and I got to where I would turn some patterns. I sat on the porch and admired it . . . and then my wife came home and I had to remow it." Fuhlendorf laughed heartily, but his point was serious. "There's no good reason why ranchers need to have that homogenized, even forage that everybody's going for," he said, running his hand across the screen to illustrate the uniform height of a "well-managed" range. Ecological research clearly shows that everybody benefits—the rancher, the animals, and the rest of the prairie ecosystem—from more variability, Fuhlendorf explained. "But we have created a culture where everybody hates noise and variability, and I think that plays into our land management. I don't think it's true for Indigenous people."

## That Which Is Given

When Latrice Tatsey returned to her field site on the Blackfeet Buffalo Ranch in August of 2020, the weather was nothing like her frigid initial visit two Junes prior. With the sun beating down relentlessly, Tatsey set up an umbrella to shade her laptop as she monitored the data generated by her LI-COR machine, watching the trendline inch up as she added soil moisture. "We use this machine to measure the amount of water and $CO_2$ the soil is respiring," Tatsey explained. "Think of it like a soil breathalyzer."

In addition to measuring respiration rates, Tatsey also gathered samples of soil in Ziploc bags, labeling them with her last name. Hundreds of miles away, in a specialized lab, a tech would generate a detailed printout of all the microscopic components of these soils, the clues Tatsey had been gathering for years. As she prepared to send her soil samples off for analysis, Tatsey wondered what else she might learn from the buffalo. Perhaps they could teach her the language of plants, what academics call chemical volatiles. Perhaps they could teach her how to best move her family's cattle so the grass regrows stronger and the animals gain more weight. So much of what her people know about how to live well in this place, she's come to realize, is due to the buffalo. "When it comes to our culture," Tatsey says, "a lot of the things that we learned were taught through these animals."

The more I spoke with Tatsey and others at Blackfeet, the more I realized that the two key practices promoted by regenerative agriculture enthusiasts were just tiny kernels of much larger and more powerful insights. The signature activity of the carbon cowboys—regenerative grazing—was mostly understood as a process of moving livestock to allow vegetation to regrow. As important a shift as this represented, it didn't get to the heart of what Latrice was telling me. Moving cows was just one lesson. The important thing was getting in the habit of listening to nonhuman relatives like the buffalo, so we could keep learning from them far into the future. While the details of agricultural management might well shift with the climate, the relationships with these animals will remain—so long as we continue to cultivate them.

The traditional food culture built around buffalo holds numerous lessons for how to live well in a changing climate, says historian Jill Falcon Mackin, who has been collaborating with the Blackfeet Nation and counts her own Plains Ojibwe ancestors among the Indigenous people who lived in close relationship with these animals for millennia. Buffalo were central to this complex and highly organized ancestral way of life, but only one of many food sources, Mackin explains. People moved across the land to find edible plants and animals and were adaptable to what was available, *when* it was available. In a sense, what made this way of life work was intimate knowledge of all that the ecosystem has to offer. "We call it *Miinigoowiziwin*, that which is given to us," Mackin told me, translating the Anishinaabe word that is the title of her dissertation. "There's this whole ethic of recognizing the gift when it's before you in the food system."

At the heart of regenerative grazing—through the lens of the buffalo and their Indigenous human relatives—is a fundamental principle, one that challenges settler agriculture to its core. To see plants and animals as gifts, and indeed as teachers, we have to let go of the idea of domination. We can no longer undermine the self-determining lifeways of some beings by placing them in the service of others as "domestic dependents." The most sustainable food systems, as the history of the North American prairie clearly demonstrates, are liberated ones.

Embracing agricultural ecosystems as communities of relatives, as the Blackfeet do, also has significant implications for the second key practice promoted by regenerative agriculture enthusiasts: no-till. Undoubtedly, excessive tillage has had disastrous consequences for soils and released over fifty billion tons of greenhouse gases into the atmosphere. Halting some of this plowing has helped reduce soil erosion. But no-till has largely failed to restore full ecosystem health because it only tells farmers what *not* to do. As State University of New York (SUNY) biology professor and ethnobotanist Robin Wall Kimmerer puts it in her book *Braiding Sweetgrass*, "all reciprocal relations [are] reduced to a 'keep out' sign."

Just as prairie vegetation has evolved to benefit from judicious buffalo grazing, writes Kimmerer, so can plants adapt to human activities. This is true for sweetgrass, which is used for ceremonial purposes both at Blackfeet and among Kimmerer's Citizen Potawatomi relatives. The aromatic perennial responds to traditional harvesting just like grasslands respond to buffalo: with compensatory growth. While learning to anticipate human "grazing," prairie plants like sweetgrass also coevolved with Indigenous burning practices. In some cases, they even learned to tolerate tillage, when people chose the time, place, and tools carefully.

Not far from the eastern edge of Blackfeet territory, the Hidatsa and Mandan people farmed the fertile bottomlands of the Missouri River for centuries, tilling the soil with carefully fashioned hand tools. Critically, the Hidatsa and Mandan only farmed low-lying areas, where the soils were renewed annually by flooding, leaving the more fragile upland prairies to the buffalo. Across the country, the Haudenosaunee people farmed for centuries as well, also using hand tools that were easier on the soil than European plows. They minimized disturbance by making semipermanent mounds to create seedbeds, so they didn't have to invert the soil each year. These Indigenous land stewards knew their soils well enough to choose appropriate cultivation tools that were minimally disruptive to soil ecology, and they waited for appropriate times and places to use them. Fully aware that their activities removed nutrients from the soil, they were diligent about giving back, whether that meant mounding up earth or allowing seasonal flooding. As their agricultural systems demonstrate, the key to farming without degrading soils isn't "no-till," but embracing reciprocity, which Kimmerer characterizes as a bedrock tenet of Indigenous ecological thought.

"Reciprocity is a matter of keeping the gift in motion through self-perpetuating cycles of giving and receiving," writes Kimmerer. "Our elders taught that the relationship between plants and humans must be one of balance. People can take too much and exceed the capacity of the plants to share again. . . . And yet, they also teach that we can take too little. If we allow traditions to die, relationships to fade, the land will suffer."

Here again, Latrice Tatsey tells me, we can learn from the buffalo. She's seen the no-till wheat farms that border the reservation, where the ground remains bare for months after each crop, starving out the soil microbes that have survived the onslaught of herbicides. She knows these soils aren't as lively as the ones she's sampling, where buffalo have grazed, trampled, and even rolled on the ground, "disturbing" it in ways that actually stimulate life. Like these buffalo, Tatsey says, people have to learn how to participate in an interdependent web of life—or else we become the broken link, the missing piece that prevents everything else from working in concert.

If the Blackfeet people fully embrace the buffalo's teachings about reciprocal relationships, Tatsey believes, they can incorporate new plants and animals into their food system too. As she tells the ranchers who've collaborated with her research, cattle can be managed in balance with this ecosystem as well. But in order to adapt to changes, the Blackfeet need the buffalo—not just to help store carbon beneath the prairie but to continuously remind the people how to thrive on that which is given. In this way, buffalo are much more than an individual food or agricultural product: they embody a food system, and an economy, within which all the other denizens of the Blackfeet Nation have a place. Like the wild rice of the Great Lakes region or the salmon of the Pacific Northwest, buffalo aren't just an ecological keystone species but a cultural keystone as well.

"These animals, they give you this constant reminder," Tatsey says, sporting a "Got Moose?" T-shirt her dad got for her on a trip to visit Indigenous colleagues in Alaska. "This is how to live well in this place."

~

Just as prairies and their Indigenous stewards play a significant role in the fate of our climate, so does another ecosystem that is currently under threat: forests. Worldwide, trees are being cut down to make way for industrial agriculture, releasing several gigatons of carbon into the atmosphere every year. Preventing deforestation and planting trees are consistently rated by scientists among the most promising and urgent climate solutions, but there's a troubling catch. As a new study has just revealed, one of the longest-running national programs to subsidize tree planting—the model used by many carbon credit schemes—has failed to achieve even modest carbon storage, and has actually accelerated biodiversity loss.

Like the prairies, however, forests have long-standing histories of sustainable Indigenous management, traditions that provide some hope of righting the climate balance. Many of these traditions come from the African continent, where trees have played cultural and agricultural roles similar to those played by buffalo on the American plains. Yet much as Latrice Tatsey's people were violently ripped from their ancient interrelationships with land, African tree stewards were also uprooted to serve the needs of settler agriculture in North America. While Indigenous Americans were dispossessed of their lands, Indigenous Africans were dispossessed of their bodies.

# CHAPTER 2
# Black Land Matters

On a humid August day in 2017, three generations of Black women drove down a backcountry road in North Carolina, a momentous decision on their minds. For 84-year-old Ruth Wallace, it was a question of whether her family's 127-year-old legacy would die with her. For her 23-year-old granddaughter, Olivia Watkins, it was a question of whether she could really make such a big commitment to a place she'd only been once before.

Raised in New Rochelle, a small urban community just north of New York City, Watkins had grown up hundreds of miles removed from her family's southern past. Though she knew they owned some land in North Carolina, the place was little more than an abstract concept to her. "To me, it was just this place out somewhere in the middle of nowhere," she says. Fascinated by science, Watkins moved to Manhattan to attend Barnard College, where she joined a soil ecology lab. Staring through a microscope, Watkins pored over the DNA structures of soil samples, transfixed by the ways such tiny organisms shaped the environment. But even more than lab work, it was fieldwork that

Watkins gravitated to, eventually traveling to the Cook Islands to conduct research on farms for her senior thesis. It wasn't long before her
interest in researching farms translated to an interest in farming herself.

"During college, anytime I had a break, I would always go somewhere to work on farms," Watkins told me. She worked a stint at an
organic vegetable farm in South Korea and a homestead in Upstate
New York. While studying abroad in New Zealand, she worked at a
citrus and kiwi orchard. Eventually, Watkins found her way to Hawai'i,
where she moved after college to work on a small mixed vegetable farm
with fruit trees. Like many of her friends in the young farmer community, she imagined managing a similar operation of her own someday.

At first, Watkins was not terribly concerned when she learned that
her grandmother was putting her family's North Carolina forestland
up for sale. Watkins had no sentimental attachment to the place, having
only been there for one brief and uneventful visit as a child. She was
looking for farmland, not forest. But just as Watkins was absorbing the
news about her family's land, she was also getting more involved with
food justice advocacy organizations. When she returned to New York to
attend a training at Soul Fire Farm—"a BIPOC-centered community
farm committed to ending racism and injustice in the food system"—
she was introduced to the concept of Black land loss as a form of systemic racism. As she learned about the obstacles her ancestors had faced
in order to purchase and hold on to their land, Watkins became less
and less willing to let it go.

## Forty Acres and a Mule?

In 1915, on the twentieth day of a wet and somewhat chilly January,
a crowd of thousands gathered at the Tuskegee Institute in Macon
County, Alabama, for the twenty-fourth annual Negro Farmers Conference. The festive occasion began at nine o'clock in the morning with

a parade, featuring twenty-four horseback riders and twenty-four bug-gies—all decked out in the official crimson and gold of the prominent historically Black college. On foot, three hundred marchers carried agricultural products, celebrating the bounty of their farms. By the end of the conference, winners of the crop and livestock exhibition con-tests would return home with up to ten dollars of prize money in their pockets.

Hundreds of similar gatherings were held across the South in the early years of the twentieth century, expressing the pride of farmers who, against all odds, were achieving their dreams of land ownership. By the end of the decade, 925,000 Black farmers owned the land they cultivated. It had not been easy.

At the close of the Civil War, as the nation wrestled with how to incor-porate nearly four million former slaves into the fabric of society, a group of Black ministers approached Union general William T. Sherman. Their request: an allotment of forty acres for each freed Black family. The general agreed, issuing Special Field Order No. 15, which would for-ever be remembered as the promise of "forty acres and a mule." Within six months, Black families gained title to some four hundred thousand acres of land in coastal South Carolina, Georgia, Florida, and the Sea Islands. For a brief moment in US history, it appeared that the formerly enslaved might indeed receive some reparation for their unpaid labor. The moment was short-lived, however, as President Andrew Johnson rescinded the order, and most of the land was seized from Black fami-lies and returned to their former enslavers. In the decades that followed, White southerners would attempt to re-create both the economic and political conditions of slavery—by any means necessary.

Many southern states passed laws prohibiting Black people from own-ing or even leasing property, part of the infamous Reconstruction-era "black codes" that outlawed voting, attending school, congregating, and "vagrancy," which was interpreted liberally so that large numbers of Black people could be arrested at harvest season and forced into contract labor as punishment. White southerners also tried to hold on to cheap agricultural labor through a debt-peonage system that looked so much like slavery that contemporary observers were often hard-pressed to describe the difference. White plantation owners offered many former slaves the opportunity to farm a portion of their land in exchange for a share of the crop, usually between 25 and 50 percent. Ostensibly, these former slaves were economically independent and could build up their savings through diligent work and lucky weather. The catch was that few of them had the means to feed and clothe their families while waiting for their cotton crop to come in, so they were forced to borrow money at exorbitant rates from local merchants—who were tightly connected to the planters whose lands they farmed. The result was often an endless cycle of debt that allowed landowners to retain their labor force indefinitely and dictate most of the terms of their work. Sharecropping, effectively a system of slavery in all but name, became the only way many capital-poor and disenfranchised southern Black people could survive financially.

Black families who did manage to acquire land were targeted, often with outright violence. More than 4,000 African Americans were lynched between 1877 and 1950, many of them landowners. An Associated Press investigation conducted in 2001 documented a devastating 150-year pattern of land theft from Black families, corroborating the dispossession of 406 Black landowners and a total of 24,000 acres. Over half the cases involved violence, the AP journalists determined, and many of the victims lost their lives as well as their land. Dozens more cases could not be verified due to gaps in the public record, the journalists lamented, and "thousands of additional reports of land-takings collected by land activists and educational institutions remain uninvestigated."

Yet Black farmers persisted, and by the turn of the century, they were literally gaining ground. By 1890, Black people had purchased 120,738 farms. By 1900, a quarter of Black farmers owned the land they farmed. And by the time the three hundred marchers at the Tuskegee Institute's 1915 Agricultural Parade were proudly displaying their produce, Black land ownership had nearly reached sixteen million acres, a full 14 percent of total farmland in the United States. Yet this historic achievement would mark not the inception of a new era of racial progress, as the Tuskegee marchers hoped, but the beginning of a devastating century of Black land loss. Over the following eight decades, 98 percent of Black landowners would be dispossessed.

First of all, Reconstruction-era practices—Jim Crow laws, racial violence, and exploitative sharecropping—continued well into the twentieth century. Then the boll weevil infestation of the 1920s decimated the cotton crop, and the 1930s brought the Great Depression. Not just Black farmers suffered from these latter two calamities, however, and the devastation to rural communities was so great as to spur the first major federal programs to support agriculture.

The devil was quite literally in the details of these New Deal farm support programs, which, on their face, ought to have been a boon to struggling Black farmers. But these programs and, critically, the low-interest loans they offered, were administered through local committees dominated by White planters whose worldviews had changed little since Reconstruction. Instead of a means of support, federal farm programs became, essentially, a means to transfer capital from the Black community to the White community. In the words of the 1965 US Commission on Civil Rights, the New Deal Farm Security Administration and its successor, the Farmers Home Administration, served to "accelerate the displacement and impoverishment of the Negro farmer."

As the Civil Rights Commission noted, many Black farmers were flatly denied the government loans to which they were entitled. Applications were thrown in the trash, unread, and Black applicants would be kept waiting for hours while White constituents were served. When loans *were* provided to Black applicants, the commission found, they were smaller than those offered to White applicants with similarly sized farms. Meanwhile, private lenders followed similar patterns of discrimination, as did lawyers and land speculators, who frequently swindled their Black clients. White tax assessors had their own scheme, jacking up appraisals so high as to force Black people off their land for inability to pay taxes.

The result of this thinly veiled onslaught of financial racism was a tidal wave of foreclosures and tax sales, which ultimately proved more devastating to Black land ownership than the violent mobs of the early twentieth century. Between 1950 and 1975, half a million Black farms went out of business, forfeiting a total of 6 million acres in the years between 1950 and 1969 alone. As journalist Vann Newkirk has calculated, this pencils out to an average daily hemorrhage of 820 acres, "an area the size of New York's Central Park erased with each sunset."

For Black families who somehow managed to maintain land over multiple generations, a new challenge arose: succession. For many in the Black community, designating specific beneficiaries in a written will was not customary—land simply passed down to descendants and was held by them in common as "heir property." Even if Black farmers had wished to write wills, few had access to the legal services necessary to create a document that would hold up in court. But without a will, heir property was vulnerable to loss. For one, it was typically ineligible for USDA programs as well as private loans. More troubling still, exploitative developers targeted heir property, hunting down distant relatives living out of state who held a share of the land—and offering them cash. Due to the flimsy legal status of heir property, a developer only needed to convince one descendant to sell, which would force the partition of the entire property to be sold at auction. Such partition sales have accounted for over half of Black land loss since 1969.

The twentieth century was undoubtedly hard on all small farmers. Rapid consolidation of the agricultural sector—fueled by "get big or get out" federal policies—pushed most family farms out of business. Between 1920 and 1997, the number of White farmers in the US declined 66 percent, a staggering loss felt as a seismic shift in White rural communities. Yet even these numbers pale in comparison to the 98 percent decline in Black farmers over the same period. Not only did Black Americans suffer more from land transfer, they were virtually never the beneficiary—as nearly all these lands are now owned by White individuals or corporations.

While the Civil Rights Commission's 1965 report failed to generate significant reform, government complicity in this mass dispossession of Black land eventually met heightened scrutiny. During the Clinton presidency, tens of thousands of Black farmers filed a class action lawsuit, demanding restitution for USDA's discriminatory administration of loans and other farm programs. In 1999, this *Pigford v. Glickman* lawsuit was settled out of court for approximately $500 million, the largest civil rights settlement in history. Payouts stemming from the case would eventually reach a total of $2 billion. While the lawsuit did much to expose and quantify the discrimination (at least during 1981–1996, the years to which the suit applied), restitution payments amounted to a small fraction of lost property value and income. "When they steal your land," commented Stephanie Hagans, the descendant of a North Carolina woman who lost her thirty-five acres to an unscrupulous White lawyer, "they steal your future."

## Legacy on the Land

As Olivia Watkins began learning about this history of Black land loss, it spurred her to dig deeper into her own family's story. Anecdotes she'd heard since childhood became invaluable clues, helping her patch together the remarkable tale of her ancestors' struggle to hang on to their land. "It's complicated," Watkins says, "because most of the knowledge is oral, but there are a couple documents here and there."

As Watkins learned, her great-great-uncle Henry Battle had been among the first wave of African Americans to buy land, purchasing eighty acres of forest in the thriving Black community of Holly Springs, North Carolina, in 1890. Few records survive from this time, so Watkins knows nearly nothing about Battle's childhood—not even the names of his parents. What she does know is that he was employed as an "office worker"—not a domestic or a sharecropper as most Black people were at the time—and that he hoped to become an entrepreneur and provide for his family. Through the racial violence of the early twentieth century, Battle and his descendants homesteaded their forest outpost, raising vegetables, chickens, and cows. It was not an easy life— they lived without running water or electricity well into the twentieth century—but it was the one place they felt safe.

As racial terror and economic discrimination continued, however, younger family members began to talk of leaving the South. Watkins's grandmother Ruth Wallace became the first in the family to go to college, then went on to earn a master's degree in home economics at North Carolina Agricultural and Technical State University. At first, Ruth and her husband, Oliver, an engineer, attempted to build a life for themselves in the South. But in the face of workplace discrimination, Oliver found it nearly impossible to get jobs, and when he started his own business, he found White clients as uninterested in his services as White bankers were in lending him money.

"There were a lot of experiences of difficulty that they felt," Watkins says of her grandparents. "My grandmother saw that and she was like, yeah, if I stay here I'm going to have a very difficult life, and she wasn't interested in that. So she asked herself, what can I do for my family to be able to continue our legacy and hold on to our land and keep it safe?"

The Wallaces made the decision to leave, finding success in an international career that took them to Japan, Greece, Thailand, and Saudi Arabia. Ruth worked as a teacher, while Oliver completed engineering projects for airports, earning enough money that they could help take care of older family members who remained on the land in North Carolina. Oliver installed electricity on the homestead in the 1950s, and he and Ruth visited frequently to check up on their relatives.

"There's a story my grandmother tells me literally every time I see her," Watkins told me, explaining the importance of these visits. "She was visiting the family who lived on the land and this White guy showed up at the doorstep and was asking my great-aunt for some land. He wanted her to write him on the deed and give him five acres. My grandma was like, yeah goodbye, get out of here. But come to find out, this guy had been coming for quite some time, asking her for land." Eventually, pressure from White neighbors forced Watkins's great-aunt to give over title to much of the land, reducing Henry Battle's eighty acres to just forty. "If there's a White guy at your door, and you're Black and you're by yourself . . . she really couldn't defend herself," Watkins explains.

Watkins's mother, a lawyer, was well aware of the swindles and legal maneuvers that caused many Black families to lose their land and hard-earned nest eggs. So she persuaded her mother to write a will, ensuring that the family would never have to deal with the "heir property" debacle. But as Watkins's grandmother approached her late eighties, it became harder and harder for her to look after the land, which was nearly three hundred miles away from her home in Washington, DC. With no one in the family prepared to take on management of the small forest, she figured it was time to put the place up for sale. And then her granddaughter asked if she could come see it.

## A Family Decision

"Can we go in there?" Watkins asked her mother and grandmother, eager to finally walk the land she'd heard so much about. There was no road going into the forest, so they'd pulled over to the side of the road adjacent to the parcel, which was lined with a thick stand of trees.

"Imagine a backcountry road and we're pulled off the side of the road and there's just like a wall of forest," Watkins remembers. "My grandmother and my mother, that was not really their thing to go into walls of forest. Especially as women, they were really worried. They did not want me to go into the forest because they didn't know what was in there." Attempting to assuage her mother's and grandmother's fears, Watkins walked carefully into the thick brush, pulling aside branches to try to get a view of the forest interior. "I got all these cobwebs in my face and there were bugs flying everywhere," Watkins recalls, chuckling. "You could tell that the land had not been walked on for a very, very long time."

While Watkins appreciated the wild beauty of the place, she also felt the loneliness of its vacancy, the stories about to be overgrown and erased. With no relatives in the area, her grandmother had nonetheless held on to these forty acres for decades, in hopes of somehow continuing the family's connection to the land that had been her ancestors' place of refuge. Watkins decided the story wasn't going to end here.

"I'm a pretty matter-of-fact person," Watkins said when I asked how she dropped the news to her grandmother that she was going to take on stewardship of the forest. "I think I said something like, 'yeah, I'm going to continue to take care of the land.' And she was like 'Thank you, Jesus!'"

## A Farm in the Forest

Less than two years later, Watkins was comfortably venturing deep into the heart of the woods, where she braced a log on her thigh to inoculate it with mushroom spawn. She posted a video of the process to her brand-new Instagram page for Oliver's Agroforest—a name she'd chosen in honor of her grandfather Oliver. Alongside the video, Watkins posted a few lines of text, explaining the purpose of her project. In one provocative sentence, she summed up the marriage between her personal path and her family's legacy. "What would it look like," Watkins asked, "for us to create farms IN the forest?"

Having chosen to farm a parcel covered with trees, Watkins decided on mushrooms for a number of reasons. She could use available resources, thinning out overgrowth to use as mushroom logs. This would allow her to get started with minimal amounts of capital and maintenance, two obstacles that can be extremely daunting for beginning farmers. Most importantly, mushrooms were a crop she could grow within the existing forest, without having to clear the land.

In North Carolina, as in most other forested parts of the world, commercial agriculture typically means cutting the trees down. In the past, this meant clearing forests to grow row crops like tobacco. Now, the diverse native forests of North Carolina are being cut down and replaced with monocultures of pine trees. In recent years, North Carolina has become the epicenter of the wood pellet industry, exporting millions of little pieces of pine to Europe as a replacement for coal. Advocates claim the process is environmentally friendly, as trees are replanted after being logged. But conservationists stress that single-species tree plantations are not the same as healthy forests, warning that much of North Carolina's biodiversity is being lost in the process. Meanwhile, rapid urbanization and sprawl in the Research Triangle communities of Raleigh, Durham, and Chapel Hill—where Oliver's Agroforest is located—has consumed considerable forestland as well. In a fifteen-year period at the end of the twentieth century, North Carolina lost over a million acres of forest to urbanization. Scientists predict another 5.5 million acres of trees will fall by 2040.

All of these trends are troubling for North Carolina's wildlife, Watkins points out, but they're also part of an even more sobering global problem. Worldwide, deforestation is predicted to cause "global biodiversity losses equaling a mass extinction." And the staggering loss of trees around the world is currently responsible for some 10 to 15 percent of global carbon emissions. As Watkins sees it, the solution is more complicated than simply protecting forests. Hands-off conservation policies, she points out, have typically created more problems than they've solved, both for people and the environment. Instead, she believes, we need to learn how to produce the food and fiber we need by drawing on the genius of forest ecosystems—working *with* trees rather than against them.

Forest farming, as Watkins is doing on her family's land, is among a suite of practices known as agroforestry—farming with or under trees. Long employed in Indigenous and traditional farming systems, agroforestry has garnered renewed attention of late due to the extraordinary capacity of trees to sequester carbon, both in their own trunks and branches and through extensive networks of roots that feed soil microbes. Trees also help buffer farms against the extreme weather associated with climate change, softening the blow of downpours and providing shade in heat waves. In addition to protecting watersheds and soils, trees provide significant wildlife habitat, attracting pollinators and beneficial insects that can help boost farm production.

Before starting Oliver's Agroforest, Watkins worked in other kinds of agroforestry systems as well. Some of the vegetable farms where she spent her college breaks had planted trees for windbreaks. The citrus and kiwi farm she worked on while studying abroad in New Zealand was entirely composed of tree crops. While in Hawai'i, she spent a year working on a farm that practiced alley cropping—interspersing rows of vegetables with fruit trees. This farm also incorporated livestock in its agroforestry system, a method known as silvopasture.

It was in Hawai'i that Watkins really came to appreciate the elegant synergies of farming with trees. In addition to the alley cropped orchard, the farm Watkins worked on had also planted several rows of vegetables with no fruit trees in between. For the curious soil ecologist, this offered somewhat of a natural experiment. "If we had a big monsoon coming through, we had to do a lot of maintenance around fortifying the soil in the row crop so we wouldn't have any soil erosion," Watkins recalls. "If it was a particularly windy day, we had to put a lot of wind barriers up. And we were always watering." In the alley cropped agroforest, Watkins noticed, the trees themselves provided a lot of these services that would otherwise require work and resources. After an initial watering in, the trees did fine with minimal irrigation, and they protected the vegetables from wind and rain. Increasingly, Watkins began to envision her farming future as a partnership with trees.

"Farming can be very stressful and unpredictable," Watkins explained. "I wanted to live a life of farming where I was adding less stress to myself, because I'm interested in farming for the rest of my life. I want to be using a system that's sustainable, for myself but also, I don't want to leave the next generation with barren and eroded soil and have them to deal with that mess."

## The Information Superhighway of the Soil

Throughout the first two years of Oliver's Agroforest, Watkins continually posted moments of delight and awe on Instagram. A turtle peeking out from under a log. A tiny waterfall. A bush teeming with butterflies. But much as she loved her regular walks through the forest floor, it was the action underground that grabbed her attention.

"I like to look at the forest as one large organism that spans forty acres," Watkins told me, explaining how trees communicate and exchange nutrients belowground. The secret, she divulged, is a vast fungal network called mycelium—the information superhighway of the soil. Individual *hyphae*—tiny filamentous parts of fungi that scavenge nutrients—join up with one another to form these mycelia, making the whole nutrient gathering operation much more successful. The mycelia don't just feed themselves but also allow trees and other plants to absorb and exchange nutrients—and send subterraneous warnings of incipient danger. As scientists have recently learned, trees use mycelial networks to communicate with one another about new threats from predators, pathogens, or toxins. This allows fellow trees to ward off the offenders by releasing deterring hormones and chemicals. Trees connected by underground fungi can even share stress signals to alert each other to deforestation.

Fungi also play an important role in cycling nutrients through the forest, Watkins explained, as they decompose decaying plants and animals so that new life can sprout. Some of this decaying matter ultimately gets stored as soil carbon, one of the reasons forests are such a powerful carbon sink. Mycelia play a key role in sequestering the massive amounts of carbon that trees gather through photosynthesis, routing these carbon stores deep below the soil surface.

The more Watkins has learned about the intricate ways in which mycelia connect individual trees to global ecological cycles, the more she's found powerful life lessons awaiting her in the woods. Compared to trees living in isolation, Watkins told me, trees living connected to one another in forests tend to live longer. It's not so different with humans, she suggested. "Mycelium is really a great teacher in terms of reminding us how collective things are," Watkins said. "There's an African proverb: if you want to go fast, go alone. If you want to go far, go together. My dad used to tell me this all the time, but I never understood until I started working with mushrooms."

## Mycelial Economies of the African Diaspora

For Watkins, stewarding mycelium goes hand in hand with the legacy of cooperative economics throughout the African diaspora. Mycelial modes of economy have a deep history in Black farming communities, stretching back through the civil rights movement and slave rebellions, all the way to Indigenous African agricultural systems. Prior to colonization, as Watkins learned through her training at Soul Fire Farm, most African lands were managed in common. Land was typically not owned, and labor was typically not monetized. This is not to say there were no hierarchies or oppressive governance systems before White people showed up, but many African societies developed sophisticated forms of collective management to sustainably steward land, which was referred to in many African languages with the same word used for *family* and *community*.

This historical legacy of cooperation proved essential to surviving the brutal kidnapping and enslavement endured by millions of Africans during the three hundred years before abolition. Mutual aid was important to everyday subsistence, as well as the organizing efforts that ultimately won enslaved people their freedom. Immediately upon emancipation, formerly enslaved people began pooling their resources to collectively acquire land. Near Georgetown, South Carolina, 160 Black families bought a former plantation and formed a joint stock company. On Saint Helena Island, 300 African families purchased ten-to-fifteen-acre parcels with the intention of establishing an independent community. According to a group of Black legal scholars who have researched this period (who themselves worked collectively to author the article), such groups acquired millions of acres of land through collective strategies, thereby "reestablishing the African village in the United States."

Such collective economic strategies were first formalized under the auspices of the Colored Farmers' Alliance, which grew from its 1886 origins in Texas to a national membership of some 1.2 million Black farmers. These early cooperative efforts blossomed into increasingly powerful institutions in the twentieth century, boosted by the impassioned leadership of sociologist W. E. B. DuBois and, later, the twin forces of the civil rights and Black Power movements. DuBois, now remembered as the first rural sociologist, was also the first scholar to research Black cooperatives in the United States. Just after writing his landmark *The Souls of Black Folk*, the prominent author and activist undertook a historical study of Black mutual aid, finding "a continuous and hidden history of economic defense and collective well-being." In his 1907 book *Economic Co-operation among Negro-Americans*, DuBois documented an underground informal economy, tracing the roots of Reconstruction-era Black social institutions all the way back to the solidarity economies of the enslaved and collective resource management systems in Africa.

Beyond studying the cooperatives of the past, DuBois sought to foster future collaborations among Black Americans, founding the Negro Cooperative Guild in 1918. The organization aimed to support Black-owned cooperatives that provided food and other necessities— such as clothing, health care, education, banking, insurance, and legal services—to their local Black community. "Tomorrow we may work for ourselves," DuBois envisioned, "exchanging services, producing an increasing proportion of goods which we consume, and being rewarded by a living wage and by work under civilized conditions."

DuBois's vision would find powerful expression in one of the most underappreciated arenas of the intersectional liberation struggles that burst forth in the 1960s: the southern cooperative movement. As historian Monica White chronicles in her book *Freedom Farmers*, this movement both drew from and bridged the civil rights and Black Power struggles, providing a common tactical foundation and a way to sustain political gains through economic means. White's book traces the stories of three influential organizations that all formed in 1967 in Mississippi, beginning with Fannie Lou Hamer's Freedom Farm.

Hamer was born in 1917, the twentieth child of sharecroppers. She was working in the fields by age six, and by age thirteen, she had quit school to labor full-time. She was struck with polio as a young woman, then forcibly sterilized when she later sought treatment for ovarian cancer, an experience she sarcastically referred to as a "Mississippi appendectomy." Thus well acquainted with racialized oppression, Hamer began registering Black voters in 1962 with the Student Nonviolent Coordinating Committee. In retaliation for her activism, she was summarily fired by her employer of eighteen years, evicted from her housing, and later arrested and beaten—for the offense of registering to vote herself. Hamer became a central figure in the civil rights movement, helping to form the Mississippi Freedom Democratic Party and pushing Congress to pass the Voting Rights Act in 1965. Based on her own experience, Hamer recognized that political freedom for Black Americans hinged on economic independence from White people, and she sought to create a cooperative institution that could provide the material foundation for liberation.

Hamer's Freedom Farm Cooperative grew into a 692-acre farm, collectively managed by 1,500 member families. Most members were Black people who, like Hamer, had lost their jobs—either due to their political activities or the increasing mechanization of agriculture, which put many sharecroppers and tenant farmers out of work. Freedom Farm included a community garden for subsistence, as well as revenue-raising enterprises such as row crop fields and a catfish cooperative. Perhaps Hamer's most significant innovation was the "pig bank," a breeding population of pigs whose offspring were given to Black families. Participating families tended to their sow—which would be bred to a boar from the pig bank—then returned two of her piglets back to the bank, keeping the rest of the litter to build up their own drift of pigs. In this way, pigs were distributed to 865 families.

Freedom Farm did not stop at agriculture. Hamer also created an eighty-unit affordable housing development, one of the nation's first Head Start programs for early childhood education, a sewing cooperative, and a tool lending library.[57] But Hamer's conception of freedom through cooperation always circled back to food. "If you have a pig in your backyard, if you have some vegetables in your garden," Hamer was fond of saying, "you can feed yourself and your family and nobody can push you around."

Freedom Farm was not the only Black agricultural cooperative formed in the South during this time. As White recounts, North Bolivar County Farm Cooperative was also launched in 1967 in Mississippi, as were dozens of similar groups. In December of that year, twenty-two representatives of these southern cooperatives called a meeting to discuss strategies for mutual support. The Federation of Southern Cooperatives—"the co-op of co-ops"—was born.

In the face of considerable resistance, the federation chipped away the financial power structure that had maintained southern agriculture's racial hierarchy ever since slavery. The federation offered loans and other financial services, so that sharecroppers didn't have to seek credit from their landlords at usurious rates. They purchased farm supplies in bulk, subverting the paternalistic "advance" system that White planters and merchants had relied on for nearly a century to overcharge Black tenants for seeds and equipment while levying exorbitant interest. The federation also collectively marketed Black farmers' crops, negotiating with buyers for better prices. By 1974, the federation was home to 134 member cooperatives from fourteen southern states, one-third of which were focused on agriculture.

In addition to financial and organizational support, the federation provided technical assistance to members and developed demonstration farms, creating what amounted to a parallel extension service. During the 1970s energy crisis, the federation constructed fourteen solar greenhouses and initiated a revolving loan fund to support farmers who wanted to install renewable energy or energy efficiency improvements. The federation also promoted and helped finance water conservation infrastructure, such as catchment systems and improved irrigation. By 1974, the organization was serving ten thousand small farmers, and by 1977, its farmers controlled one million acres of land.

Perhaps the most telling evidence of the federation's success was the reaction of the White power establishment in the South. White elites took extraordinary measures to undermine the federation's power, boycotting their products, convincing a congressman to call for a federal audit of their books, and aggressively lobbying the Office of Economic Opportunity to stop giving them grants. In a particularly blatant attempt to suppress the cooperative movement, Alabama state troopers stopped a fleet of refrigerated trucks delivering produce for the Southwest Alabama Farmers Cooperative Association. The troopers released the drivers but detained the trucks until they ran out of gas and the cucumbers inside rotted.

Nonetheless, the federation and the cooperatives it represents have continued their work, now over fifty years strong. Other Black cooperative institutions live on as well. For example, New Communities, a 5,700-acre collective farm founded in 1969 by civil rights leaders Charles and Shirley Sherrod, continues its legacy as the nation's first community land trust. Though the farm folded due to discrimination from USDA lending programs, the Sherrods won the largest settlement in the *Pigford* lawsuit, using the money to purchase a former plantation and rekindle their vision. While organizations like New Communities continue to serve Black farmers in the South, similar cooperative strategies have traveled with Black people who have moved to northern cities. Over the course of the twentieth century, informal mutual aid networks linking backyard gardens grew into more formalized twenty-first-century organizations such as Karen Washington's Garden of Happiness in New York, the Detroit Black Community Food Security Network, and Oakland's Mandela Grocery Cooperative.

At Oliver's Agroforest, Olivia Watkins also prioritizes community, participating in the Black Farmers Market in Durham and hosting work parties and skill-sharing sessions for folks curious to give mushroom farming a try. When considering potential crops to add to her operation, she looks for what might best complement the produce offered by her neighbors. "We have so many great vegetable farms in the area," she told me, "so I don't see any reason to duplicate that."

Meanwhile, Watkins works to encourage mycelial networks belowground by managing her farm to fit the forest, rather than the other way around. Unlike many of the surrounding properties with timber on them—which tend to be nothing but pine trees—Oliver's Agroforest contains a diverse mix of hardwoods—yellow poplar, oak, sweetgum, maple, black cherry, American beech—in addition to a few shortleaf and loblolly pines. As a result, Watkins's farm provides valuable wildlife habitat and ecosystem services, which she's eager to preserve, even as she produces food on the same land.

Once she got mushrooms established, Watkins's next venture was beekeeping—another enterprise that works well under the trees. When she's gotten the hang of honey, Watkins is planning to add shade-tolerant perennials like elderberry, persimmon, currants, pecan, and hazelnut. To get those plantings started, she'll use mulch from her spent mushroom logs and water from the stream that runs through the center of the parcel. Meanwhile, she's making the most of her shady work environment, which can be quite a relief in a climate where summers are typically hot and muggy. "It just wouldn't make sense for me to cut down forty acres of trees to put row crops in," Watkins told me. "It's just not necessary."

While Watkins's forest-inspired farm management approach is a bit of an anomaly in the US, even among organic farmers, she's far from alone. In many ways, her climate-friendly strategy of forest farming draws on a long legacy of Black agroforestry and learning from the woods.

## A Misunderstood Forefather of Regenerative Agriculture

One of the key figures in this history of forest-inspired agriculture is George Washington Carver. Arguably the first US scientist to reject industrial farming and call for regenerative organic approaches, Carver has been hailed by a recent biographer as "a prophet of sustainable agriculture." However, this was not how he was perceived by his contemporaries in the early twentieth century. Though Carver would become "the most widely recognized and admired Black man in America," his fame hinged on his role in the commercialization of peanuts and his largely mythological status as a path-breaking chemist, leaving his legacy of regenerative agricultural research virtually unknown.

Carver was born into slavery in Missouri, likely in 1864. His father was killed in an accident before his birth, and he and his mother were kidnapped when he was a baby. Carver's mother was never found, but young George was rescued, and he was raised by his former enslavers in the early days of abolition. Frail, orphaned, and facing an uncertain future, Carver found solace in the woods, where he became something of a self-taught naturalist. "I literally lived in the woods," Carver recalled in 1922. "I wanted to know every strange stone, flower, insect, bird, or beast." His adoptive mother began requiring Carver to empty his pockets before entering the family house, concerned about how many "specimens" he was bringing inside. But he had a space of his own to tinker—a hidden wildflower garden in the woods where he experimented with transplants.

Carver eventually made his way to Simpson College in Indianola, Iowa, where he enrolled in 1890. He had been there for just one semester when his painting teacher, Etta Budd, noticed his affinity for plants and recommended he pursue a degree at the Iowa Agricultural College in Ames, where her father, Joseph, was an eminent horticulture professor. Carver was not only the first Black student to attend the Iowa Agricultural College (now Iowa State) but quite possibly the only Black person in Ames. Unable to find a White family willing to board him, he got permission to stay in an empty office in exchange for serving as the building's janitor.

As he negotiated the challenges of integrating a midwestern farm community, Carver devoted himself to his studies. Perhaps most significantly, he was introduced to the emerging field of ecology by professor Louis Pammel, author of the first book in English to use the new scientific term in its title. With Pammel's encouragement, Carver stayed on at the college to pursue a graduate degree.

While Carver is remembered as the "peanut man," his early interest was in mushrooms. Though he had no prior scientific background in mycology, he reportedly arrived at the college with significant knowledge of fungi from his rambles in the woods. A young cook at Ames recalled sharing in the bounty of mushrooms that Carver gathered on walks and prepared in his room. Pammel quickly picked up on Carver's capacities as a collector of fungi, and the two coauthored a pair of articles in mycology journals. Carver also collaborated with one of Pammel's former students, F. C. Stewart, who worked as a mycologist at the New York State Agricultural Experiment Station. Primed for a career as a mycologist, Carver began dreaming of a PhD. He was discussing his prospects with Pammel when Booker T. Washington wrote to offer Carver a position as the head of the Tuskegee Institute's new agricultural school.

Washington, the founding president of Tuskegee, was the leading Black public intellectual of his time, and his institute was the best-known Black school in the country. For Carver, who had pursued scientific agriculture because he believed it was his God-given duty to spread this knowledge for the uplift of his people, this was an offer he couldn't refuse. After all, Carver was the only African American who held an advanced degree in agricultural science at the time.

## The Poor Farmer's Scientist

When Carver arrived at Tuskegee in 1896, the thirty-two-year-old scientist was placed in charge of the institute's new agricultural experiment station and its outreach activities to Black farmers, eventually helping to develop a "moveable school." In the early years of his career, he would also manage the university's 2,300 acres of farmland and teach up to six classes a semester.

Unifying all these activities was Carver's singular vision: to foster the liberation of Black folks through the practical application of ecology. As biographer Mark Hersey writes, Carver "intended to show the impoverished tenant farmers of Macon County and the Cotton Belt exactly what to look for in the natural world. If he could open their eyes to that, he could show them how to win their economic independence—and free themselves from the worst of the injustices they endured on account of their race."

Best remembered among the ecological practices Carver promoted (again, thanks to the peanut story) is the rotation of "pod-bearing plants"—leguminous crops in the bean and pea family that convert atmospheric nitrogen to natural fertilizer. Though he extolled the virtues of peanuts, Carver was perhaps even more enamored of the cowpea (or black-eyed pea)—an indigenous African legume brought to North America by enslaved people and little known at the time. In a 1903 extension bulletin, Carver lauded the two-toned legume as "absolutely indispensable in a wise crop rotation," and provided twenty-five recipes for dishes featuring the protein-rich bean.

In addition, Carver promoted building up soils by planting non-harvested "green manure," or cover crops, as well as using animal manure. Assessing the ten acres set aside for his new experiment station—former plantation land that had been poorly farmed and suffered from devastating erosion—Carver quickly determined that it was in much the same condition as many of the soils farmed by sharecroppers and the few Black landowners in the region. By necessity, his first experiment, beginning in 1897, would be a demonstration of how to restore healthy soil on degraded land. Mulching and manuring with gusto, Carver poured organic matter into the tired earth, utilizing barnyard manure, plant residue, and soil-building crops. By 1905, he had managed to curb the erosion, and students began taking note of the dramatically transformed field.

In the early 1900s, practices like composting and cover cropping were not alternative or countercultural; in fact, they were considered mainstream tenets of scientific agriculture. Seaman Knapp, founder of the USDA county agent system and arguably the most influential agricultural scientist at the time, included both practices in his "Ten Commandments of Agriculture," which also promoted crop rotation. But as the field of agricultural science—and its connections to industrial agriculture—grew, recommendations for applying chemically compounded commercial fertilizer increasingly eclipsed discussion of organic methods. A full three decades before J. I. Rodale founded his famous farm and began publishing *Organic Gardening* magazine, Carver was one of the first agricultural scientists to question US agriculture's turn toward chemicals, initially on the grounds that the farmers he served could not afford them.

In 1900, nearly 95 percent of Black farmers were tenants or sharecroppers who cultivated land owned by White landlords. Fertilizer application at the rates his colleagues were recommending in the early 1900s, Carver calculated, would cost $720 for a twenty-acre farm—far more than any White landlord would loan to a Black tenant. Even if they used just a fraction of the recommended rate, chemical fertility could easily cost more than the tenant was likely to earn from their crop.

To Carver's frustration, many of the organic fertility strategies he advocated were beyond reach for poor Black farmers as well. Crop rotation and cover cropping were out—so long as cotton markets were good, landlords expected their tenants to dedicate every acre to the lucrative cash crop. Most sharecroppers couldn't afford well-bred livestock, meaning they had no source of animal manure. Theoretically, they could borrow the money, but any attempt to get ahead or become economically independent was looked upon with suspicion by local White merchants and planters who provided the only source of credit.

Recognizing that the scientific agriculture he had learned in Iowa was of little use to the farmers he hoped to serve, Carver turned to his original source of inspiration: the woods.

## A Forest of Riches

As he had in Iowa, Carver foraged the woods for wild plants and mushrooms, encouraging others to do so as well. "Nature has provided us with an almost innumerable variety of wild vegetables," he wrote in a 1938 leaflet, "which serve not only as food, but as medicine." Carver also continued the mycological collection work he had begun at Iowa Agricultural College. A 1902 *Journal of Mycology* article entitled "New Alabama Fungi" lists sixty species collected by Carver, including two new species named after him, *Colletotrichum carveri* and *Metasphaeria carveri*.

But Carver looked to the woods for more than just food and mycological specimens. His very first bulletin at the Tuskegee experiment station, for instance, promoted the use of acorns as feed for livestock. Noting the value of the free and nutrient-dense nuts, he entreated his readers to protect the trees from land clearing. "We hope the days are not far distant," Carver wrote, "when the destruction of our valuable oak forests will cease." Carver also harvested walnut, pecan, beechnut, and hickory nuts, suggesting in a 1916 circular that they might be made into cakes and sold for a little off-season income. He was likewise full of ideas for how wood could be used: chairs, tables, shingles, baskets, tool handles—all of which could be useful at home or sold in town. "We are richer than we think we are," he told Black farmers.

If Carver appreciated the woods as the Black farmer's provider, this belief was bound up with his equally strong conviction that the forest was his people's most helpful teacher. Woods provided instruction not only in the "organic unity" of the ecosystem and the "mutual relationship of the animal, mineral, and vegetable kingdoms," as Carver espoused, but also provided countless examples of how to do more with less, by using what nature provided. A walk through the woods, Carver wrote, was a walk through a "natural fertilizer factory," which produced "countless tons of the finest kind of manure, rich in potash, phosphates, nitrogen, and humus, all of which our soils are badly in need of."

Hence, it was the decaying leaves of the woods that eventually led Carver to the solution he would forever after promote as the poor Black farmer's salvation: compost. This organic fertilizer, easily generated with materials readily available to even the most economically marginalized Black sharecropper, would become the scientist's primary focus. Carver put composting at the center of his research program, studying the breakdown rates of various locally abundant plant materials, from crop residue to "swamp muck." He reported astonishing improvements in the water-holding capacity of his fields following compost application[107] and became somewhat of a missionary for the humble soil amendment, declaring it "Nature's choicest fertilizer."

At one point, Carver even tried to get the entire Tuskegee campus to switch from commercial fertilizers to compost for managing its farms and grounds. In a 1911 letter to Booker T. Washington, Carver asked for support to hire students to help him rake up manure, and went so far as to suggest composting human waste. The scheme could possibly pay for itself, he proposed, as "the expenditure for commercial fertilizers should grow less every year." Carver had come to recognize that chemically compounded fertilizers weren't just unaffordable for Black farmers, they were likely a bad idea for wealthy White farmers too. "We know that commercial fertilizers will stimulate and for a while produce good results," Carver wrote to Washington, "but by and by a collapse will come, as the soil will be reduced to practically clay and sand."

Washington failed to act on Carver's recommendations, and a year later, Carver brought the request to Tuskegee's council. As justification for the proposal, Carver referenced his compost research, citing "his recent report that he raised two bales of cotton on [one and a half] acres of land . . . using a compost of leaves, muck and barnyard manure." But in contrast to his vocal promotion of compost in his bulletins, Carver beseeched the council "that his name be not used in the matter." By 1912, going against the chemical dogma of his colleagues could undermine his credentials as a scientist.

Though Carver failed to get the Tuskegee farm to adopt composting, his work to promote ecological farming did help some Black farmers improve their land and gain a foothold in the agricultural sector. In the first ten years of the twentieth century, Black farm ownership in Macon County—where Tuskegee was located—grew by a factor of three. Nonetheless, Carver understood that the formal economy was stacked against Black farmers in ways that were unlikely to subside quickly. Consequently, he simultaneously promoted a parallel and hidden Black subsistence economy—a food system fashioned by and for Macon County's predominantly African American population, in symbiosis with their bounteous woods. If Black people could not always win with cash crops, Carver reasoned, they could nonetheless enjoy "a good plate of dandelion greens . . . or . . . wild onions, seasoned and fried" and perhaps save themselves having to borrow money from their landlord for dinner. To the end, Carver remained convinced that his life's work was to be an ecological educator, just as he'd explained in his acceptance letter for the job at Tuskegee. "This line of education," Carver wrote to Booker T. Washington in 1896, "is the key to unlock the golden door of freedom to our people."

## The Deep Roots of Black Agroforestry

While Carver's career marks the beginning of resistance to chemical agriculture, the roots of Black agroforestry stretch back hundreds and perhaps thousands of years. When Olivia Watkins chose to farm with and around the trees of Oliver's Agroforest—rather than cutting them down—she found herself drawing on strategies that originated in Africa.

Prior to slavery and colonization, African Indigenous agriculture was as diverse as the continent itself, ranging from pastoral systems in arid regions to diverse savanna farms that developed over one hundred different crops, including sorghum, okra, watermelon, tamarind, and hibiscus. Trees were central to African Indigenous farming, not only producing fruit and nuts but also providing oil, medicine, fiber, and what scientists call "ecosystem services"—ecological functions like shade, habitat, and erosion prevention. On the African savanna, farmers protected a number of valued tree species, planting their crops around them rather than cutting them down. Among these species were the locust bean, baobab, oil palm, and the shea nut tree, which served as a source of both cooking oil and moisturizer. In the tropics, African farmers intercropped vegetables, grains, and trees in multiple layers, creating a multitiered canopy structure that mimicked natural forest cover and buffered the soil from heavy rainfall that could otherwise cause erosion. As geographers Judith Carney and Richard Rosomoff put it, these farmers "[transformed] a rainforest into a food forest."

Agroforestry systems in Africa developed into highly complex assemblages of diverse plants, fine-tuned to complement one another and make the best use of available resources. African farmers pruned tree crops to allow adequate light for crops planted below and also identified shade tolerant crops that could thrive under a thick canopy. As Soul Fire Farm cofounder Leah Penniman notes, Ghanaian farmers have developed numerous polycultures of trees and row crops, as have the Hausa farmers of Nigeria, who utilize at least 156 systematic crop combinations.

When Africans were enslaved and transported to the Americas, many reestablished their agroforests as "dooryard gardens" for daily subsistence. Braiding seeds into their hair before the brutal Middle Passage, Africans brought staple foods with them, intercropping them with indigenous American plants that they incorporated into their dense, multilayered home gardens.[123] Dooryard gardens introduced black-eyed peas, oil palm, hibiscus, okra, and African tubers and rice to the New World, while integrating local foods like plantains and various fruit trees. Maize and peanuts—crops that had long thrived on both continents—were frequently planted in the gardens of the enslaved, as were multiple varieties of leafy greens and medicinal herbs. White observers marveled at the bounteous gardens which "produced at all seasons," and were "always intermingled with fruit trees." One missionary recorded more than eighteen different intercrops being grown by enslaved people in the Virgin Islands in 1768.

Dooryard gardens were not only reservoirs of cultural survival and food security. As geographer Carney points out, they were also "islands of agrobiodiversity disrupting a sea of commodity monoculture," providing refuge to the nonhumans displaced by the plantation system as well. These subsistence food forests, Carney and Rosomoff write, served as "the botanical gardens of the Atlantic world's dispossessed."

In short order, however, home agroforests and forest gardens would help their stewards transform dispossession into resistance. Forest foods and medicines figured prominently in the lives of "maroons"—escaped slaves who founded independent communities, often in the woods—and provided critical nourishment to fugitive slaves on their way to freedom. Harriet Tubman, the famous leader of the Underground Railroad, was a longtime student of the forest, where she worked on a timber gang as a young woman. Tubman's knowledge of wild plants and herbal medicine proved crucial in her ability to guide runaway slaves on long journeys through the woods, and she also used her skills to heal Union soldiers in the Civil War.

## The Plantations Are Back

These agroforestry traditions of Africa—and diasporic Black resistance—stand in sharp contrast to the single-species tree farms currently expanding around the globe. This worrying trend—particularly the rapid planting of oil palm across Indonesia, Brazil, and Colombia in recent years—bears a troubling resemblance to the colonial agricultural systems of centuries ago. Once again, anthropologist Tania Murray Li writes, monocultural crops are being used in a "predatory system," compelling people to exploit both land and other people in order to survive. As Li puts it, "the plantations are back."

Perhaps even more disturbingly, this plantation model is also permeating global tree-planting campaigns intended to combat climate change and store carbon, such as the Bonn Challenge and Trillion Trees Initiative. With so many of these planned afforestation projects designed as monocultures, researchers warn, it's unlikely there will be climate benefits—and they may actually create more problems than they solve. "If policies to incentivize tree plantations are poorly designed or poorly enforced, there is a high risk of not only wasting public money but also releasing more carbon and losing biodiversity," says Stanford professor Eric Lambin, who recently coauthored a study on a long-standing afforestation subsidy program in Chile that has been used as a model for other tree planting policies and projects. The net impact of this Chilean afforestation program, Lambin and his colleagues found, has been replacement of biodiverse and carbon-rich native forests with profitable tree plantations. Since the Chilean government failed to adequately differentiate between these two very different types of forest (and elites successfully shaped the program to meet their needs), the policy has failed to increase carbon storage and has accelerated biodiversity losses.

Olivia Watkins is well aware that the regenerative potential of trees and forests can literally be undercut by plantation logic and the shadow of colonialism, which is why she chooses her words carefully. I once listened in as Watkins described the process of inoculating logs with mushroom spores for a webinar series on agroforestry, explaining why she uses the term "spawn run" to describe the fungi's association with the log. "Some people call it colonization," she acknowledged. "But I don't like that word."

When I asked Watkins to elaborate, she explained that colonization connotes violence, and that's not how mycelia—strands of fungi that collaborate to form a sort of superorganism—operate. "It's important to be mindful in the language that we use," Watkins continued "and actually observe this relationship that mycelium and mushrooms have with the logs, rather than projecting a colonial model onto it that then impacts how we manage them."

## A Black Agrarian Revival

For Watkins, decolonization is an everyday practice, as she learns how to be in relationship with this land, mycelium-style. Instead of imposing a farm, she asks the woods which foods she should raise, allowing her business to evolve like the successional stages of a forest. Even choosing which trees to thin for mushroom logs has been a deeply intentional process for Watkins. First, she studied which trees were most important as food and habitat for wildlife. Then she observed places where these sustaining trees were getting choked by other species—and thinned out those.

It's all part of the forest stewardship plan Watkins is working on, with partners from the North Carolina Forest Service and Natural Resources Conservation Service. Her family has long had a forest management plan on file with the Forest Service, Watkins explained, but the stewardship plan is something different. "The current plan is basically a plan in terms of best practices for how to take care of a forest for the end use of timber," she told me. "But the goal with the forest stewardship plan is to focus not only on the end benefit of products but also on the end benefit of wildlife in the area. That is a completely different way of looking at the land."

As Watkins works to regenerate this particular piece of land, she's also part of a blossoming movement of young Black people reclaiming pride in their agricultural heritage. This network of Black agrarians stretches across the African diaspora, from the Deep South to the northernmost reaches of New England, as well as several points west and even outside the United States. Some, like Watkins, farm land that their family acquired and retained against all odds. Others, who often describe themselves as "returning generation" farmers, are coming back to agriculture after several generations of disconnection from the land, leasing or purchasing acreage in the communities where they now live. Joining forces to push for policy change, these young Black farmers have been central to major new federal legislation. Working hand in hand with Senator Raphael Warnock, they helped ensure that the American Rescue Plan (the pandemic relief bill passed in early 2021) included the $5 billion he proposed for farmers of color: $4 billion in debt relief, as well as an additional $1 billion to help underrepresented farmers secure land, technical assistance, and legal support. They were also central to developing many of the policies contained in the Justice for Black Farmers Act proposed by Senator Cory Booker, including a provision to provide land grants of up to 160 acres to both current and aspiring Black farmers. "We're those folks whose ancestors left the land," says Soul Fire Farm cofounder Leah Penniman, "and we're realizing that along with that very understandable departure there was a bit of our culture and souls left behind in those soils that we want to go reclaim."

No one knows for sure just how many young Black folks are currently farming in the US, Penniman says, because USDA census figures exclude both farmworkers and urban farmers, leaving many farmers of color uncounted. But some 500 to 800 people attend the annual Black Farmers & Urban Gardeners Conference, she says, and her own organization alone trains a couple thousand farmers of color each year—and still has a long waiting list. "When we did a webinar during COVID, specifically for Black farmers, there would be about 1,200 attendees," Penniman says, adding with a chuckle that this was not the case when she started farming in 1996. "Back then, when I went to farming conferences, it was not unusual for me to be the only Black person in the room."

Penniman and Soul Fire Farm are undoubtedly among the most powerful nodal points of this Black Agrarian revival, enthusiastically convening like-minded organizations to collaborate and lobby policymakers, while helping aspiring young farmers like Olivia Watkins plug in and find their own role in the growing movement. After attending Soul Fire's weeklong beginning farmer training, BIPOC FIRE (Black Indigenous People Of Color Farming In Relationship with Earth), Watkins applied for a full summer of apprenticeship on the farm.

"It was very notable that Olivia showed up to her working interview dressed appropriately," Penniman recalls. "And by dressed appropriately, I mean she had a full set of rain gear and muck boots, and we were so impressed by this." Not all applicants to Soul Fire's programs have a realistic picture of farming, Penniman has learned. "A lot of people's idea of farming, even after they've been to a permaculture course or something, is that you are prancing around barefoot in the field harvesting greens or something," she says, laughing. "Olivia showed up on a cold day and she was ready to go."

The Soul Fire team was so impressed with Watkins, in fact, that they elected her to their board of directors. Not long after, she was tapped to be the founding president of a closely allied organization, the Black Farmer Fund, which works to capitalize farmers like those who've trained with Soul Fire Farm and Farm School NYC (a BIPOC-centered farming education program that focuses on urban agriculture). By providing low-interest loans and grants, and supporting a network of farms and food businesses with financial coaching, Black Farmer Fund puts Watkins's mycelial philosophy into practice, shifting philanthropic and investment norms along the way. When I spoke with Penniman, she explained that she had recently talked to a donor who was interested in supporting Black farmers but overwhelmed by the prospect of choosing which projects to fund and concerned that funding one group but not another could create conflicts. "So they're like, where can we put this huge chunk of money and y'all sort it out," Penniman recalled. "To have an actual entity like Black Farmer Fund, that is set up with the mission of receiving these thematic donations and then letting the people closest to the issue decide on what's needed and how to distribute it—that's the holy grail of democratized funding and it's encouraging philanthropy to approach us differently."

## A Patch of Survival Space

Speaking with Watkins and Penniman reminded me of a central concept in conservation ecology, developed by ecologists John Vandermeer and Ivette Perfecto. Working in highly biodiverse tropical forests, Vandermeer and Perfecto have spent decades observing the impacts of agriculture on these critical ecosystems. When they began doing this work, most of their colleagues assumed that raising food was inherently destructive to the ecosystem. The best strategy for conservation, most scientists insisted, was to limit the extent of agriculture as much as possible.

But Vandermeer and Perfecto observed a more nuanced picture. Recently arrived industrial agriculture—where large areas of forest were clear-cut to make room for soybeans or cattle or sun-grown coffee—was indeed destructive. Yet traditional forms of agriculture, which popped up in patches within and around the forest, did not eradicate wildlife or destroy healthy ecosystems. Running a number of mathematical models on different patterns of land use, Vandermeer and Perfecto came to see the issue, quite literally, from a bird's-eye view. What birds and other migratory wildlife needed, they determined, were corridors they could move through to reach the resources they required. That is, not all of an animal's territory had to provide a complete habitat. These creatures just needed enough life-giving patches to get from one place to another. This mosaic of patches—characteristic of traditional agricultural systems that disturbed some areas of forest while letting others regrow—was what Vandermeer and Perfecto came to refer to as "nature's matrix."

Oliver's Agroforest, I started to see, was one such corridor, a patch of survival space actively integrating itself into the larger matrices of Black agrarianism and the agroforestry movement. For generations, people facing oppression had found safe passage here. In turn, they maintained a sanctuary for the forest-dwelling creatures of this rapidly urbanizing region. "This is a place where my family found freedom and self-sustenance and survival," Watkins told me, "but for me it's also about broader survival for the Holly Springs area, where a lot of wildlife are trying to survive because their homes are being destroyed."

In direct contrast to the plantation model, Watkins demonstrates a forestry of mutual uplift, a forest that celebrates difference and allows for many forms of life to coexist. In ecological terms, a matrix. Or in the words of the Combahee River Collective, "If Black women were free, it would mean that everyone else would have to be free since our freedom would necessitate the destruction of all the systems of oppression."

~

As Watkins stewards forest habitat and Black agrarian legacies in North Carolina, another budding soil ecologist digs into similarly complicated histories in California's Central Valley, untangling intertwined threads of life giving and life taking. Her people too were wanted for their agricultural labor, but denied a place in society. They too were ripped away from deep histories of interconnection with the lands they left behind. And much like the freedom fighters of the Black diaspora, they quietly sustained their agrarian traditions in the cracks and edges of the oppressive system they struggled against, planting seeds of regeneration and renewal.

# CHAPTER 3
# Hidden Hotspots
# of Biodiversity

There were days during Aidee Guzman's dissertation field research when the temperature in California's Central Valley spiked as high as 110 degrees, a visceral reminder of global climate change. Guzman (whose first name is pronounced "eye-day") worked during the cooler morning hours for the pollination phase of her study, rising at four o'clock to count bees at sunrise. But she was also interested in microscopic fungi belowground, so she had to time her fieldwork carefully to avoid sweating it out with an auger while digging up soil samples.

One of the first images I saw of Guzman on social media, posted by her then-labmates at UC Berkeley, featured the five-foot-two scientist nonchalantly digging a soil pit while wearing a blazer and lace-up black boots, her dark brown hair pulled back in a ponytail and her hoop earrings gleaming in the sun. Moving deftly between different contexts has become something of a trademark for Guzman, who pulled triple duty as her lab's lead graphic designer, resident stats whiz, and one of the main authors of the group's antiracism statement. Now a postdoctoral fellow at UC Irvine, Guzman splits her time between interviewing farmers, sampling soils, and sequencing the genomes of tiny fungi. "Really, she's one of the most badass people I've ever met," says Guzman's former labmate Paige Stanley.

Guzman's raw energy is a force of its own. Ideas spill out of her mouth a mile a minute, a punk-rock-speed mixtape of research hypotheses, campus politics, and outtakes from punchy grad students exhausted after long days in the lab. But then she stops midsentence to note the presence of a native bee, and you realize that this is a person who can sit for hours by herself in a field without saying anything.

Guzman was among hundreds of agricultural researchers collecting soil samples that summer in the Central Valley, one of the most intensively farmed regions in the world. One-third of the produce grown in the United States is raised in this valley, mostly in massive industrial monocultures. Corporate vegetable farms here have long relied on tight relationships with university researchers and consultants who can take soil samples and tell them how much chemical fertilizer to apply. But Guzman wasn't working on corporate farms, nor was she interested in offering fertilizer prescriptions. Her research would record the *untold* story of Central Valley agriculture: its hidden hotspots of biodiversity.

Tucked between giant tracts of pistachios and processing tomatoes, Guzman found, are some two thousand small farmers who raise their crops on less than 1 percent of the valley's total acreage. Some of these farms are extremely diverse, growing as many as one hundred crops on as few as five or ten acres. Guzman wanted to know if these tiny oases of biodiversity might be enough to make a difference to threatened pollinators—and the beneficial microorganisms that play a key role in soil health.

Guzman built research partnerships with thirty-one small farmers, half of whom were growing a single crop, and half of whom grew a diverse mix. Guzman compared the two farm types, systematically observing bees and taking nearly four hundred soil samples. What she saw in the lab was astonishing: though they were surrounded by acres upon acres of dramatically simplified and degraded landscapes, the small diversified farms were literally bringing the land back to life.

## Unlocking the Secrets of Soil

The first signs of life were the bees. Guzman found an increase in pollinators of all kinds on the diversified farms in her study, including some species she didn't expect. She assumed that squash bees—which, as their name implies, rely exclusively on squash to provide pollen for their young—would gravitate to fields full of nothing but their favorite vegetable. But even these specialist squash bees preferred polyculture to monoculture. Once the squash flowers closed for the morning, Guzman observed, bees in the polycultures stuck around to forage other crops for supplemental nectar, while bees in squash monocultures had nothing left to eat.

Guzman's primary interest, however, was in the biodiversity she couldn't see, the biodiversity that will likely determine whether farming can continue in this valley in the context of a changing climate. Using recently developed DNA sequencing technology, she hoped to get a glimpse into the little-known world of soil microbes, and specifically, a microscopic fungus that's been associating with plant roots for some five hundred million years. These arbuscular mycorrhizal fungi, Guzman explained, played a key role in helping plants make the evolutionary leap from the ocean onto land. The two symbionts have been collaborating ever since: the plants provide carbon (a.k.a. energy) to the fungi, and the fungi extend their threadlike hyphae through the soil to forage for nutrients and water that the much larger plant roots can't access. Nearly 80 percent of terrestrial plants—including most major food crops—associate with these arbuscular mycorrhizal fungi, or AMF. Early research has shown that the presence of these fungi can help plants better cope with drought, and the AMF appear to provide protection against pests and diseases. They also seem to play a role in several processes key to storing carbon underground, including nutrient cycling and the formation and aggregation of soil.

But despite the omnipresence of these fungi and the critical role they play in the ecosystem, researchers are just beginning to understand how they operate. "These fungi can perform a whole host of other functions that we don't actually understand that well," says Guzman's PhD advisor Tim Bowles, who also studies AMF. "But we have some ideas." One of those ideas has to do with diversity *within* the AMF community, which, as Guzman stresses, is crucial for soil health. On the industrial monoculture farms that border her study sites, the soil is constantly being disturbed and is left bare for long periods between crops. All these conditions starve out arbuscular mycorrhizal fungi, which rely on plant roots for their food and thrive on a diverse diet. The only AMF that can survive here are the selfish ones, which exploit and hoard resources without giving much back to their plant hosts. Guzman calls these selfish AMF the "ruderal taxa," and explains that this is essentially what we've selected for with industrial farming. Research conducted in natural areas, however, shows a much greater diversity of AMF, which in turn is associated with all the potential soil-building and climate benefits that have made these mysterious fungi a subject of interest. Guzman wanted to know if diversified farms with dozens of different crops might look *just enough* like a natural environment—to a microscopic fungus—that they could attract this more diverse AMF community.

The process of finding out was laborious. Guzman had to meticulously identify and analyze the DNA present in the soil, sequencing it to create a full picture of which types of AMF were present. The whole procedure took more than a year, but the results were worth it. Polyculture fields turned out to have some two times as many types of arbuscular mycorrhizal fungi compared to their monocultural counterparts,

Guzman found, including rarer types of fungi not often found on farms. "So the implication," Guzman told me, "is that if we want biodiversity belowground, which I would argue is essential for soil health and climate response, we need biodiversity aboveground."

There's another layer to this story of diversity begetting diversity: all the small farms participating in Guzman's research are managed by immigrants, many of them from Mexico and Central America. While there are thousands of such farms in the Central Valley, they typically fly under the radar of official agricultural institutions, so Guzman had to get creative to recruit farmers for her study. First, she used satellite images to identify densely planted polycultures amid the sea of almonds and grapes in the Fresno area. Then she started knocking on doors. Guzman visited with over a hundred farmers, asking them for basic information about their operations and requesting permission to sample their soil and observe bees. Few of the farmers spoke English, and even fewer had ever gotten such requests from a university researcher, despite the fact that some had been on their land for decades. Their presence had simply been ignored by academics, Guzman lamented, leaving a gaping hole in scientists' understanding of Central Valley agriculture.

These farms differed from their neighbors in numerous ways, Guzman noted. They were frequently run by women. They tended to grow foods that couldn't be easily obtained in a major supermarket, often from seeds they had brought with them from their homelands. And many of their fields bore a striking resemblance to one of the most ancient polycultural farming traditions in the world: the *milpa*.

## Planting the Seeds of Their Ancestors

When Indigenous Mesoamerican people first domesticated corn, some five thousand years ago, they knew better than to grow it alone. By itself, this highly productive grain would rapidly use up the nutrients in the soil, particularly nitrogen, and large stands of it would be attractive to pests, which might decimate the crop. So alongside corn, people planted beans, which could gather nitrogen from the atmosphere and provide their own fertility. They also planted squash, which covered the ground with its broad leaves, protecting against erosion and smothering weeds. The squash even contained special weed-suppressing chemicals in its leaves, which leached out during rainstorms. Together, the corn, beans, and squash made the most of the sunlight, each catching the sun's rays at a different angle. The complex three-dimensional structure of the intercrop provided habitat for beneficial insects, while confusing pests. As farmers have long known and researchers have confirmed in recent decades, the whole really does add up to more than the sum of its parts: the total yield of this polyculture outperforms the combined yields of the three crops when they are grown by themselves.

After originating in what is now Mexico, this three-sisters polyculture—the *milpa*—spread throughout what anthropologist Devon Peña terms the "indigenous corn belt," from South America to the northeastern part of what is now the United States. In each place, people saved seeds from the plants that fared best in their environment, creating a vast diversity of milpas adapted to arid plateaus, tropical rainforests, and cool mountain valleys. Though corn, beans, and squash were the staples, many other plants were incorporated into these dense polycultures: peppers, tomatoes, herbs, cacti, and a variety of perennial and wild species. As a team of Mexican ecologists wrote in a recent analysis, the milpa has "played a key role in the maintenance and regeneration of biological diversity" while providing "the foundation of food security in many Latin American rural communities for centuries."

Guzman observed several plantings of corn, beans, and squash in the fields where she conducted her research. This was one of the reasons she chose squash as a focal crop for her study: because it was so commonly grown. But the most biodiverse parts of these farms—the true hidden hotspots—were the home gardens that families maintained for their own consumption. "Even the monoculture farms," Guzman said, "if they lived on the property they often had all kinds of things growing in their garden."

Guzman told me the story of one such farm, a former horse ranch surrounded by miles of almond orchards. Because the place had been abandoned for over a decade, the farmer had been able to purchase it—making him one of the few collaborators in Guzman's study who both owned and lived on his farm. This definitely gave him a different relationship to the land, Guzman said. "There were oak trees in and around his fields," Guzman told me, "which you would never see on one of the large-scale farms in the Central Valley. The farmer told me he decided not to cut them down because they were really pretty."

When she first looked at the farm, all Guzman saw was eggplant. This was the only crop he knew how to sell in the commercial market, the farmer explained, since he'd delivered eggplant to packinghouses as a farmworker. But closer to the house, Guzman saw a host of other vegetables, including *nopales*—the edible cacti that are a staple of Mexican American home gardens. The garden was for his own family's use, the farmer told Guzman, and he also sold the surplus to local Mexican American and immigrant families. On her way out, Guzman noticed a farmstand along the country road, stopping just long enough to read the sign: "*vendemos elotes, nopales . . .* " (we sell grilled corn on the cob, cactus . . . ). "Honestly," Guzman says, "there were so many vegetables on there that I can't remember."

The history of such home gardens dates back over ten thousand years ago to the beginnings of agriculture in the Americas. Archaeologists have found their remains up and down Mexico and Central America, with some of the oldest seeds—including avocado, prickly pear cactus, and mesquite—appearing in a cave in the Tehuacán Valley, in what is now the Mexican state of Puebla. Initially composed of a mixture of wild plants and "incidentally" domesticated species, these home gardens folded agriculture seamlessly into the landscape. In the indigenous languages of Nahuatl and Maya, ecologist Francisco Rosado-May explains, there is no word that directly corresponds to the English word *agriculture*. "In Maya," Rosado-May writes, "the closest expression is *MeyajbilK'aax*, which means working with nature."

This practice was perfected by the Mayans, whose multilayered home gardens developed into some of the most complex agricultural landscapes in the world. At the ground level, these gardens were anchored by root crops, like cassava and *camote*, a type of sweet potato. The three sisters were typically present as well, with squash providing ground cover and beans providing nitrogen fertility for corn. Fruit trees formed a lower canopy layer, with native trees above them in the upper canopy. Small livestock such as turkeys, chickens, and pigs might be incorporated into the system too. "The best way to think about these gardens from an ecological standpoint," Guzman explains, "is to understand them as a forest."

Home gardens like those of the ancient Mayan people have persisted among Indigenous and peasant communities in Mexico, and contemporary research has established that these gardens do indeed replicate the structure and function of the surrounding rainforest. They are extremely biodiverse (including more than eighty plants used by people, according to one study), full of perennial species, and as leafy and dense as a forest. For the people who tend them, these gardens offer a comprehensive grocery store and pharmacy, and yet to a bird or an ant, they are simply rainforest habitat.

As Guzman observed, home gardens have also traveled with Mexican people who have migrated to the United States, appearing everywhere from backyards in Seattle to median strips in Los Angeles to the edges of Vermont dairies staffed by Mexican American farmworkers. Heidi Liere, an ecology professor at Seattle University, was amazed to see them in a small community garden in Santa Cruz, California, right next to the surf destination's famous waterfront boardwalk. Liere, originally from Guatemala, has spent years studying the ecological properties of small farms in Guatemala and Mexico, so she's well acquainted with polycultures. But this one took her by surprise. "You're right there by the roller coaster, and suddenly you find yourself in the middle of a milpa," Liere recalls of her first visit to the Beach Flats Community Garden. "The majority of gardeners there are Central American and they brought all their knowledge with them." Liere's research in urban gardens like Beach Flats is documenting the connection between cultural diversity, plant diversity, and insect diversity, showing that gardens like this one have more beneficial insects, which in turn support pest control.

But for the most part, the thousands of Mexican American home gardens scattered across the US go unnoticed. "They flourish in hidden spaces, they're not front and center," says Gabriel Valle, an anthropology professor at California State University San Marcos. Valle spent four years interviewing gardeners in San Jose, many of them undocumented, who were growing food in tiny, dense plots behind gates and fences. "You wouldn't know that these gardens existed unless you're invited," Valle says. As Valle indicates, agricultural researchers have been missing these hidden hotspots of biodiversity for decades, passing them over to work on large monoculture farms with easily controlled variables. But Guzman has known about them all her life.

## Between the Garden and the Fields

Born in the Central Valley to farmworker parents, Guzman watched her dad attempt to re-create some semblance of their family's diverse small farm in rural Mexico, taking cuttings of nopales and planting them whenever he landed somewhere for a few weeks for a job. She heard stories about her dad and her uncle trying over and over again to get their corn and pepper seeds established in chilly Washington State, where they migrated for the apple harvest. Guzman bounced around different government housing developments as a toddler, before her parents landed in a home of their own in Firebaugh, California, when she was three. "It was a rural housing project," Guzman recalls. "The deal was, we'll give you the materials and if you build it, it's your house."

Guzman remembers her mom immediately starting a garden, which became one of her favorite places to play. But she was increasingly aware that a very different kind of agriculture was dictating the rhythms of her family's life. "My first impression of agriculture was my parents having to drop me off at a stranger's home to be taken care of because they had to go work in the fields really early," Guzman recalls. "And I'll never forget the smells they came home with—their clothes smelled like rotting vegetables."

At first, both Guzman's parents worked temporary jobs. Harvesting melon. Weeding tomatoes. Cutting asparagus. Some days, Guzman's mom would get up extra early to board a bus bound for the Salinas Valley, where she would pick lettuce all day before getting back on the bus for the two-hour ride home. Then Guzman's dad caught a break, picking up a consistent job on a sheep and cotton farm near their family home. He was originally hired to do odd jobs, laying out irrigation pipes and making repairs. But when the tractor driver quit and the boss asked if anybody could step in, Guzman's dad volunteered. "He didn't actually know how to drive a tractor," Guzman says, giggling as she tells the story, "but he got on and just started figuring it out."

As a tractor driver, Guzman's dad got paid a little bit more. Having gotten his residency through the amnesty process established by the 1986 Immigration Reform and Control Act, he was working toward citizenship. But his boss was "full-on racist," Guzman said, which could make the job miserable. "I was in the same grade with the boss's daughter," Guzman recalls, "and she was the same way. I still see her on Facebook sometimes, and of course she's a proud Trump supporter."

It was hard for Guzman to understand why her dad would put up with such treatment. But he kept telling her about the family's land back in Mexico, and how he had to send money back to his relatives so they could keep the farm. "So of course I wondered," Guzman recalls. "What's so special about this farm?"

At last, when she was nine years old, Guzman got the chance to see the farm where her dad grew up in Mexico. Her mom packed their family of six into a van and drove them 2,300 miles southeast, passing through Southern Arizona and New Mexico before crossing the border in Laredo, Texas. From there, the Guzmans still had another 700 miles to go, passing through several Mexican states before finally arriving in Hidalgo and heading out into the country, toward Aidee's uncle's home in the town of El Pedregal. "The moment we got there, the world opened up," Guzman remembers. "I could see the canyon. People were harvesting. The food. My family. The animals running around. I thought it was beautiful."

Nestled into the side of a canyon in Mexico's transverse volcanic mountain range, El Pedregal is home to several hundred *campesinos* (small farmers) who farm the plateau above the town. Chili peppers originated close by, and the town also features numerous endemic species of cacti, which has led to the establishment of a biosphere reserve. The arid, sloping landscape is what most agricultural scientists would call marginal. But Guzman's family has been growing food there for generations, without irrigation.

Guzman vividly remembers the first time she woke up at five o'clock in the morning with her uncles and followed them up to the fields, quickly getting winded as she made the mile-long trek "straight up." The scene before her on the top of the plateau was nothing like the massive stretches of grape vines and almond orchards back home in the Central Valley. Her dad's field of corn and beans was nestled in between several small plots managed by other people in the family and community. Depending on the slope of their plot, each family planted their rows in different orientations to best catch the precious rain. Squash plants were dotted throughout the landscape, as were a number of flowers that her uncles taught her to eat. "That really struck me," Guzman remembers. "You would never see random flowers popping up in the middle of the growing season in the Central Valley."

On the edge of the fields were three perennial species. There were nopales, which were harvested periodically both for their succulent pads and their refreshing fruits, or *tunas*. Alongside these edible cacti were agaves, the leaves of which were used to prepare barbacoa—the signature slow-cooked meat dish of Central Mexico, traditionally steamed in an underground oven. And most farmers had also planted *huisache*, an acacia tree that could be used for firewood.

"When I got to graduate school and started learning about all the ecological benefits of hedgerows, I thought, 'that's really fascinating,'" recalls Guzman. "I realized these plants I'd seen on my family's farm were preventing erosion, which is really important on this previously volcanic land. My dad will talk about it too. If somebody's not properly securing their land, he'll say 'that farm's fucked because they haven't planted huisache.'"

In addition to their field up on the plateau, Guzman's family maintained a garden next to their house, which was basically a living pantry. There were corn and beans here too, as well as a specific variety of squash, *tamalayota*, that had long been a family favorite. Guzman recalls an astonishing variety of herbs and tomatoes as well—"basically everything you need to cook with."

For certain key ingredients, however, Guzman's dad would walk out to "*la sierra*," the wild country surrounding the house. He knew about the hundred-year-old avocado trees growing alongside the stream that ran through the town, and he showed Guzman where to look for wild greens. But the most prized treasures were the *chiltepines*: tiny, intensely hot wild *chiles* that are the ancestors of today's commercial pepper varieties. "What's interesting about this pepper," Guzman says, "is that it needs some degree of shade. So my family would start trimming things until it had the perfect amount of shade. Or if it wasn't producing and they thought it was too hot, they would create little shade structures for it."

As Guzman continued to visit her family over the years, she came to appreciate the rhythm of life in El Pedregal. How her uncle always planted after the first rain. How the community would go around and bless all the fields at that time, in the name of a particular saint. ("I forget which *santito* it is because I'm not very Catholic," Guzman admits). How everyone got involved in the "huge" harvest at the end of the year. But mostly she noticed how much it all meant to her dad. "It's just this little piece of land," Guzman says of her family farm in El Pedregal. "But he's really attached to it."

As little bits of her family's history surfaced, one story at a time, Guzman began to appreciate why the farm meant so much to her father. His grandfather, she learned, had worked on a large plantation, or *hacienda*, in the early 1900s. "There are stories about when they would harvest corn," Guzman tells me. "They would take some of the seeds home and they would hide them so they could plant some food for themselves." After the early twentieth-century Mexican Revolution, Guzman learned, land was redistributed into *ejidos*: community-governed farmlands divided into individual parcels managed by particular families. According to the revolution's popular slogan, "*la tierra es para el que la trabaja*" (the land is for those who work it). So her grandfather, the former plantation worker, received a plot of thirty acres.

"My great-grandpa suffered so much for us to have this land," Guzman says. "So my dad doesn't want to lose it. In the ejido system, if you don't take care of your land, it can be taken away. So all this time, my dad's been sending money home just so my family can stay here."

From this point, Guzman pours out the whole story: how the actions of the Mexican and US governments tanked corn prices, undermining her family's livelihood. How her dad and her uncle began crossing the border to earn money as farmworkers. How one by one, her aunts and uncles kept coming too, reeling from the triple blow of drought, genetically modified seeds, and the North American Free Trade Agreement. And through it all, how her dad kept sending money back, determined not to let go of the farm. As Guzman's story illustrates, the diverse communities identified as "Latino" have been on the front lines of industrial agriculture—and leading calls for reform—for nearly a century.

## A New Science, with Ancient Roots

In the late 1940s, a young Mexican scientist by the name of Efraím Hernández Xolocotzi set out to collect corn seed. Born in 1913 in Tlaxcala, which he would later describe as "the smallest and perhaps the poorest state in Central Mexico," Xolocotzi moved to the United States as a youth and earned a bachelor's degree in applied agriculture at Cornell University. The budding scientist impressed his professors and was accepted to a graduate program at Harvard University, where he began to study economic botany. But in the late 1930s, Xolocotzi abandoned his PhD program to return home to Mexico, preferring to work directly with farmers in his home country. He held a variety of short-term government jobs in agriculture before the disruption of World War II left him temporarily unemployed.

Xolocotzi got his big break when he was offered a position with the newly formed Mexican Agricultural Program of the influential Rockefeller Foundation. The program was seeking genetic material for its corn breeding efforts, and it was Xolocotzi's job to collect as many varieties as he could find.

When Xolocotzi joined the Mexican Agricultural Program, the initiative was at a contentious crossroads. The idea for the program had been hatched a decade earlier, just as then–Mexican president Lázaro Cárdenas was implementing a massive land reform, attempting to fulfill the promise of the 1917 Mexican Revolution. Cárdenas ultimately redistributed over twenty million hectares, establishing a new communal land tenure structure called the *ejido*. By 1940, nearly half of all farmable land in Mexico was held in these ejidos.

Though the prospect of such a land reform may sound beyond the pale of the mainstream US political imagination, many contemporary US observers were strong admirers of the ejido system. Frequently sincere in their determination to eradicate poverty, New Dealers and progressive philanthropists saw redistribution of resources as a means of blunting violent revolt and deeper challenges to elite power. Consequently, influential figures within and around the Rockefeller Foundation dreamed up the Mexican Agricultural Program: a technical assistance effort in support of the new *ejidatarios*, to help them build secure livelihoods on their land.

The program's original scientific team focused on "inexpensive and feasible" methods of increasing staple crop yields, accessible to rural small farmers. Composting, crop rotation, and soil-building cover crops were their preferred methods for boosting fertility, with commercial fertilizers as a last resort. In breeding crops, they sought to produce seeds that could be saved and replanted by farmers rather than needing to be purchased each season. And critically, they focused on corn: the primary crop grown by small farmers across Mexico, often for their own subsistence as well as a modest income.

But in the late 1940s, an array of forces joined together to push the Mexican Agricultural Program in a dramatically different direction. Cárdenas's successor Ávila Camacho—who had been sympathetic to land reform—was replaced in 1946 by new Mexican president Miguel Alemán, who was far less enthusiastic about the ejido system. In contrast to the early Rockefeller scientists, who insisted that any genetic improvement must produce seeds that farmers could reproduce themselves, Alemán preferred "hybrid" seeds that did not "breed true" and thus had to be acquired anew each year. Such hybrid varieties were becoming popular with seed companies in the United States, which recognized a profitable business model. Alemán liked them for a similar reason—if farmers became reliant on the government as a source of seed, that would ensure their political loyalty.

But the strongest force pushing on the Rockefeller program came from beyond Mexico's borders. As the Cold War battle between the United States and the Soviets heated up, global food security emerged as an urgent political issue. Influential public intellectuals warned that hungry people were vulnerable to communism and urged the United States to deploy food aid and agricultural assistance as a "weapon." Meanwhile, prominent conservationists published best-selling books projecting massive global food shortages, heightening the sense of urgency to raise yields in the "Third World." The Mexican Agricultural Program, which had begun as an effort to help small farmers in Mexico, was abruptly asked to provide a universally replicable model for how to feed the world.

In this context, a young plant pathologist at the Mexican Agricultural Program began advocating for dramatic funding increases to the program's wheat breeding initiative. The pathologist, Norman Borlaug, was frustrated with his superiors' focus on small farms, which he believed were "not economical." Born and raised in Iowa, Borlaug had come to Rockefeller after working for agribusiness giants like DuPont, and he was confident he could use his skills to deliver high-yielding grains if only his colleagues would let him. After threatening resignation, Borlaug won the support he was looking for, establishing a new research center in the heart of the northern Mexican wheat belt. Unlike corn farmers, Mexican wheat farmers were mostly wealthy elites, often had ties to US industry, and were both willing and able to achieve Borlaug's vision for high-input, export-oriented agriculture. Working hand in hand with these massive estates, Borlaug bred hybrid wheat seeds that produced incredible yields—when managed with irrigation, herbicides, and heavy doses of commercial fertilizer. Under enormous pressure, this approach was adopted by the Rockefeller corn breeding program as well, and soon exported to Colombia, India, Chile, and the Philippines. Borlaug would win the Nobel Peace Prize in 1970, credited with saving the world from mass starvation through his "Green Revolution."

But Xolocotzi had his doubts. As the young botanist crisscrossed the indigenous corn belt in the late 1940s and '50s, journeying across rural Mexico, Guatemala, Colombia, Ecuador, and Peru, he did indeed find the incredible diversity of corn genetics the Rockefeller Foundation was seeking. That the plants would be diverse was unsurprising: Xolocotzi was traversing four of the ten most biodiverse countries in the world, in the "Center of Origin" where corn was first domesticated from its wild ancestor.

And yet what most struck Xolocotzi wasn't the seeds themselves but the people who had been selecting and planting them for generations. When he asked about corn, farmers volunteered an encyclopedia's worth of information about their distinct varieties: what elevation to grow them at, which might fare better in a dry year, which made the best tortillas, and of course, how to grow them in polyculture with beans and squash (which his informants figured must be essential if the goal was yield). Increasingly, Xolocotzi strayed from his stated mission to gather "raw material" from these supposedly backward peasants for whom Norman Borlaug had such disdain, pouring equal effort into recording farmers' instructions for how to tend their plants. The real treasure of rural Mexican agriculture, Xolocotzi realized, wasn't its genetic material. It was its people.

The Green Revolution, Xolocotzi observed, was not useful to the majority of Mexican farmers. What good were "improved" seeds if they required chemical fertilizers, pesticides, and irrigation that peasants and Indigenous people couldn't access? What good was a hybrid bred for the lowlands to a farmer living five thousand feet above sea level? Xolocotzi became more and more dubious about the efforts his seed collection was supporting as he watched the saga of agricultural development play out. Wealthy farmers, using chemicals and irrigation subsidized by Rockefeller and the Mexican government, exploited Mexico's lowlands, churning out record-breaking yields. Prices fell and markets dramatically restructured, undercutting the very small farmers who had so generously shared their seeds with Xolocotzi, believing in his humanitarian mission. Xolocotzi watched in horror as these small farmers were squeezed out of their livelihoods, jeopardizing not only one of the world's greatest living archives of agricultural diversity but millennia of knowledge about how to raise these plants in balance with their surroundings. The star recruit of the Mexican Agricultural Project started speaking out.

Xolocotzi, who'd been appointed to a prestigious professorship at the National School of Agriculture in Chapingo, just outside Mexico City, was supposed to teach plant taxonomy and economic botany. But by the end of the 1960s, he was pivoting strongly toward ethnobotany and ethnobiology, or as he put it "the mutual relations between man and plants." Xolocotzi began speaking proudly about his Indigenous Nahuatl heritage and questioning the doctrine that Mexico needed to be modernized. Meanwhile, just seven miles down the road from campus, the Green Revolution was deepening its grip on Mexican agriculture, as the International Maize and Wheat Improvement Center (CIMMYT) was established in 1966. The distance between "Maestro Xolo" and his colleagues widened into a yawning gap, and the increasingly frustrated professor began searching for a new word to describe the kind of agriculture he believed Mexico desperately needed to conserve.

In 1976, Xolocotzi held a national seminar on the "Agroecosystems of Mexico," publishing the proceedings the following year. The term *agroecosystem* had been used as early as the 1930s, periodically appearing in scientific journal articles about the ecosystem properties of farms. But in Xolocotzi's parlance, the term gained a normative dimension. He wasn't just observing agricultural ecosystems, he was making the case for a more ecological agriculture, based on traditional farming knowledge. In 1978, Xolocotzi cohosted an even more pointedly titled seminar, "Agroecosystems with an Emphasis on the Study of Traditional Agricultural Technology." This event was not held in Chapingo, but at a tiny, four-year-old college of tropical agriculture in southeastern Mexico.

The Colegio Superior de Agricultura Tropical, or CSAT, had a lot in common with Xolocotzi's home institution. It too was meant to be a mouthpiece of the Green Revolution, having been placed intentionally in the midst of a two-hundred-thousand-acre Inter-American Development Bank project. The project intended to clear the forest, drain the wetlands, move the area's inhabitants into cement-block houses, and get these locals planting monocultures of corn using Green Revolution seeds and chemicals. Working in concert with the Mexican government, the bank hoped to turn the region into "the new granary of Mexico," with a focus on export crops. The college's job was to provide technical assistance and solve any problems that might arise.

Yet the founding director of CSAT, Ángel Ramos Sánchez, took a decidedly ecumenical approach to the school's curriculum. Sánchez was an agronomist, but he'd completed a master's degree in botany, focused on tropical grasses. And his master's advisor? Efraím Hernández Xolocotzi himself. Like Maestro Xolo, Sánchez was proud of his Indigenous heritage, which he identified as Mixtec. Sánchez believed agricultural scientists needed to understand the natural environments where they worked, so he created an ecology department and hired several young scholars to teach ecosystem science to agronomists.

The team of young ecologists bonded, taking in their new surroundings as they made the thirteen-mile drive back and forth from the college to the town of Cárdenas, Tabasco. On one such trip, an ecologist from California named Steve Gliessman was carpooling with a Mexican plant pathologist named Roberto Garcia Espinosa. Garcia Espinosa wasn't technically an ecologist, Gliessman recalls, but the pathologist "understood that instead of continuing to focus so much attention on getting rid of diseases once they had become problems, we needed to see disease as a problem inherent in the design of agricultural systems." As the two men drove up to the college, they noticed a healthy-looking corn planting in an area that had been fully inundated with water just a few months earlier. Curious, they got out of the car and started talking to the farmers tending the field. The farmers began describing an intricate strategy for farming on seasonal wetlands, explaining how they squeaked in a corn crop during the brief spring dry season. Gliessman and Garcia Espinosa were introduced to the keeper of these fast-maturing *marceño* seeds (the seeds of March), who was over a hundred years old and still tended to his own small *huerto*, or home garden. The "healthy-looking" corn crop, they would eventually learn, was yielding some five to ten times the conventional average—with no fertilizer.

The experience had a profound effect on the two researchers, who became deeply concerned about the Inter-American Development Bank's plans to drain such wetlands. They wondered why no one else at the college had bothered to pay attention to the traditional Mayan agriculture that was all around—not only scattered across the margins of the development project, but even tucked into the unoccupied parcels within it. The scientists began stopping to talk to farmers more often, setting up experiments to document the ecological functioning of their fields. They came to believe that these farmers' approaches were far more effective than the ones being promoted by their own institution, and they started conducting studies with the farmers to prove it.

When these ecologists teamed up with Xolocotzi and his research group at the 1978 Agroecosystems seminar, the environment was electric. Unlike a typical academic seminar, the meeting was packed with farmers, whose voices were front and center in the discussion of participatory research approaches. An international summer course was established at CSAT that very same year, as was a new master's program. It was called agroecology.

The new discipline spread rapidly throughout Latin America. An agroecology course similar to the one at CSAT was launched at Colombia's national university by Ivan Zuluaga and Miguel Altieri, the latter of whom would publish a Spanish-language agroecology textbook in 1982. Both Altieri and Gliessman would take up teaching positions in the United States, founding agroecology programs at UC Berkeley and UC Santa Cruz. John Vandermeer and Ivette Perfecto would establish a similarly influential program at the University of Michigan. And eventually, a graduate student named Aidee Guzman would join the lab of Altieri's successor at Berkeley, fostering a new generation of agroecology.

## Ecological Engineers Ahead of Their Time

Meanwhile, in Mexico, the researchers who'd been present at the 1978 Agroecosystems seminar set to work. They conducted thorough studies of milpas, documenting everything from the nitrogen-fixing capacity of the beans to the weed-suppressing activity of the squash. They counted species and measured leaf cover in tropical home gardens, comparing their results with the properties of the surrounding forest. These early Mexican agroecologists also turned their attention to the wetland agriculture that Gliessman and Garcia Espinosa had so fortuitously stumbled upon. During the nine months that these fields were covered in water, the scientists found, marsh vegetation grew and decayed, creating soils with 30 percent organic matter. (For reference, a typical industrial farm has about 1–2 percent organic matter, while a well-managed organic farm might reach 5 percent). This steady input of organic material made for extremely fertile soils, as well as a heck of a lot of carbon stored in the depths of the marsh. But when the fields were artificially drained in an attempt to prolong the growing season (as the Green Revolution scientists counseled), the thick mat of organic matter was reduced to just two inches in less than two years, causing yields to plummet.

Agroecologists uncovered other fascinating forms of wetland agriculture too, including a raised field system in Xolocotzi's home state of Tlaxcala. Here, in the Puebla Basin floodplain, farmers had mounted an elegant community engineering project to cultivate the swampy soils. As Gliessman and his student Tim Crews observed, farmers had excavated massive trenches of soil, forming long, narrow raised fields surrounded by drainage canals. The fields—now elevated enough to avoid flooding—were planted with the same sort of diverse polycultures agroecologists had observed in more typical milpas. Some 10–30 percent of the crops in the raised field were nitrogen-fixing legumes, including climbing beans intercropped with corn, as well as bush beans grown separately. The farmers had also incorporated a nonnative perennial legume—alfalfa. The deep-rooted forage provided fodder for livestock, and the animals' manure was returned to the field as nitrogen-rich fertilizer.

On the edges of the fields, farmers planted a variety of trees, particularly alders. The tree roots stabilized the soil on the sides of the drainage canals, preventing erosion, while the falling leaves of the nitrogen-fixing alders added yet more fertility to the land. Irrigation was built into the architecture of the system too: the surface of the raised fields was still close enough to the water table that moisture could simply travel up to the plant roots through "capillarity"—the miracle of physics that allows water to move through narrow spaces in the soil via surface tension alone.

What most struck Gliessman and Crews, however, weren't the fields but the canals between them. These trenches combined the functions of an irrigation ditch and a compost pile, while virtually eliminating nutrient runoff. Supplying water in the dry season, the canals also built up marsh vegetation that decayed into rich layers of organic matter, much like the seasonal wetlands Gliessman had observed over a decade earlier with his colleague Roberto Garcia Espinosa. In Tlaxcala, farmers actually added to this reservoir of organic matter, tossing unwelcome plants into the canals when weeding. Every few years, the community gathered to dredge the canals, piling the stored fertility atop the fields. The result, Gliessman and Crews concluded, was a farming system that was "largely self-reliant in energy and nutrients."

Other agroecologists documented a similar network of raised fields in urban Mexico City: "floating gardens," or *chinampas*. These artificial islands in the middle of Lake Texcoco and nearby lakes in the Mexico City region had been constructed in much the same way as the raised fields in Tlaxcala. Soil had been excavated from the bottom of the shallow lake and piled up to create a rich garden bed. Aquatic plants—particularly water hyacinth—provided continuous organic matter, ensuring the soil stayed fertile. Originally developed by the Mayans in the tropical lowlands and later adapted for upland conditions by the

Mexica (or Aztecs), they were part of a once vast network of raised field systems that stretched throughout Central and South America.

Prior to the arrival of the Spanish, chinampas provided most of the food for the dense human population in the Mexica capital, which was home to hundreds of thousands if not millions of people. In 1519, the year Hernán Cortés arrived in present-day Mexico City, the chinampas produced one hundred million pounds of corn. The Spanish drained most of these wetland gardens, but there were still enough chinampas remaining in 1930 to supply most of the vegetables for the one million people then living in Mexico City. In the words of one scientist, chinampas were "one of the most intensive and productive production systems ever developed."

To agroecologists, these ancient urban "floating" gardens provided a model of ecological farming. In addition to supporting "renewable" soils, chinampas created microenvironments that protected crops from frost. The raised gardens also hosted fungi that prevented the spread of pathogens, and they sequestered significant quantities of carbon.

That last quality has led to recent calls to revive the chinampas—as a strategy to curb the emissions caused by rampant draining of wetlands. Praising the original architects of the chinampas as "ecological engineers ahead of their time," scholars note that these raised fields managed to produce huge amounts of food while keeping the wetland ecosystem and most of its vast carbon stores intact. This "working wetlands" strategy might ultimately prove far more effective than conservation alone, ecologists suggest, "[locking] away large quantities of carbon from the atmosphere for millennia."

The people who first built the chinampas were not concerned with climate change, of course, but they were highly aware of the importance of soil health. The Mayans distinguished between soils with different textures and levels of fertility, while the Mexica recognized some sixty different soil classes, based on properties like organic matter levels, permeability and moisture retention, sensitivity to compaction, and susceptibility to erosion. The Mexica had a general term for soil that was appropriate for cultivation, *cuenchihu*, as well as a term for soil that had been degraded by careless farming practices: *tepetate*. More fundamentally, the Mexica recognized soils as living organisms and felt an obligation to care for them. This made a great deal of sense. Prior to the arrival of the Green Revolution and its chemical fertilizers and pesticides, it was the biological health of soils that formed the basis of Latin American agriculture for thousands of years.

## Traditions Uprooted

Despite the monumental efforts of Xolocotzi and company, however, the Green Revolution did arrive, with devastating impacts on traditional farming systems in Mexico. Whole families abandoned their rural villages. Agrobiodiversity declined. Formerly self-sufficient in corn, Mexico became a net importer of the staple grain by 1970. Food prices began to rise. Thousands of displaced peasants like Aidee Guzman's parents sought work as farm laborers in the United States, where they were systematically denied full citizenship.

These dynamics were exacerbated in the early 1990s under the administration of Mexican president Carlos Salinas. In 1991, Salinas formally ended the ejido system of communal land tenure, and in 1994, he signed the North American Free Trade Agreement (NAFTA), prompting a deluge of government-subsidized US corn onto the Mexican market. Corn imports from the US spiked to twenty times their previous level. Corn prices fell $160 per ton. And as the number of Mexican corn producers fell by one-third, corn-producing regions began to contribute outsized numbers of migrants to the United States.

"In the 1990s and the 2000s, that's when most of my cousins came to the United States," recalls Guzman. Initially, her dad and her uncle were the only ones among twelve siblings to migrate north of the border for work, as most of the family stayed on the farm. But as corn prices fell, life in El Pedregal became more and more difficult. Somewhat desperate, people were grateful when the government began handing out bundles of corn seeds in the 1990s, Guzman says. But the genetically modified seeds—bred for irrigated lowland farms—were unprepared for the drought that plagued Mexico for the next decade, and campesinos' harvests were decimated. Caught in a triple bind of drought, GMOs, and NAFTA, many of the Guzmans and their neighbors were forced to move. "I have these vivid images from my childhood of visiting our family who had just come to the US," says Guzman. "They were living in this semi-empty warehouse . . . some of them were in a trailer park. And they all worked in the fields."

Some one million small farmers would be uprooted by the disruptions associated with the first decade following NAFTA and the demise of ejidos, with devastating impacts for the plants and people left behind. In 2005, a researcher visited a rural village in southeastern Mexico where an anthropologist had once recorded the biological diversity of local milpas. In 1960, the original study found as many as thirty-two different kinds of plants growing in a seven-and-a-half-acre plot. By 2005, there were just eight.

And yet, as Guzman's research demonstrates, neither these plants nor the knowledge associated with them disappeared. Instead, they were frequently transplanted to the United States, where farmworker activism became a new front in the fight for agroecology. Long before organic food went mainstream, the United Farm Workers (UFW) raised consumer awareness about pesticides, describing how they jeopardized the health of both workers and the environment. Strict regulation of chemicals was among the terms demanded by UFW negotiators, whose contracts are cited by historians as "the first effective oversight of pesticides."

Alongside the overt activism of the United Farm Workers and the Chicano movement arose a quieter form of resistance. People smuggled seeds across the border and shared them with one another. Vacant lots suddenly sprouted milpas. In the midst of an industrial agricultural system, in a country that demanded their labor but refused to grant them citizenship, people quietly planted spaces of sanctuary and survival.

Now, after decades maintaining tiny garden spaces while laboring in other people's fields, increasing numbers of Mexican Americans and other immigrants from Central and South America are managing their own farms. Even the USDA's Census of Agriculture—which is widely believed to undercount these farmers due to insufficient outreach in immigrant communities—has registered this trend. According to these census figures, the share of US farms owned by people who identify as Hispanic or Latino increased 21 percent between 2007 and 2012, and Hispanic-operated farms increased another 8 percent between 2012 and 2017. The pressures of the industrial food system continue to weigh on these farmers, some of whom are forced to replicate the monoculture plantings of their former employers in order to earn a living. But as Guzman has documented, many of them are bringing a different form of farming to the landscape, a form that is sorely needed in the face of climate change.

## These Are Not Weeds

As Guzman's research highlights, the cornerstone of these Latin American regenerative agriculture traditions is their extremely high levels of biodiversity, even within a single planting. This core principle of Indigenous Mesoamerican farming, I learned, goes far beyond the notion of "diversifying crops." The idea that individual crops must be somehow combined or diversified doesn't make sense in a context "where polyculture is the default," says Ricardo Salvador, a former Iowa State University agronomist of Zapotec heritage who now directs the Union of

Concerned Scientists' Food and Environment Program. In Latin America, farms have long been understood from the outset in terms of crop *communities*, as exemplified by the word *milpa*. The term doesn't mean "cornfield," though it is sometimes translated that way. Rather, *milpa* (derived from the Nahuatl term for field) refers to the entire complex of which corn is just one part. The beans that vine around it. The squash that spreads out beneath it. The wild plants that stabilize the soil. It is literally unthinkable to plant a single "crop" by itself. "There wouldn't even be a term for a corn monoculture in the Nahuatl language, nor in the other native languages I'm familiar with, Zapotec and Lacandón Maya," says Salvador. "A field of *just corn*? What is that?"

Polycultures like the milpa are central to rebalancing the climate and preventing mass extinction, Guzman tells me, emphasizing that science is just beginning to catch up with the farmers who have been managing ecological synergies for millennia. She shows me two hand-digitized maps created by her research assistant Christina Fuentes, who generated colored GPS polygons for each crop in Guzman's study of Central Valley farms. The first map is simply a big blob of purple—a monoculture. But the second explodes with ribbons of color. This, Guzman says, is what bringing soils back to life looks like.

Guzman reiterates her research results, which show that plant diversity aboveground directly corresponds to microbial diversity belowground, fostering soil health and the processes that help sequester carbon. And then she shares another fascinating tidbit. Commercially available seeds, Guzman explains, have not been selected to emphasize plants' capacity to associate with the beneficial fungi she studies. This is a legacy of Green Revolution–style plant breeding: seeds are typically bred in environments with so much access to chemical nutrients that the plants don't bother to seek out the microbial partners that help them forage nutrients in the soil. In addition, plant breeders frequently use fungicide, which kills beneficial fungi as well as potential disease. By interrupting this five-hundred-million-year-old symbiosis and making it standard practice for plant breeders, we've likely been selecting *away* from plants that cooperate well with beneficial soil fungi. To what extent this is true, researchers don't know—no one has been tracking this. But what we do know is that the seeds used by many of the farmers Guzman is working with—as well as her own family—have been selected very differently, mostly in the context of polycultures, where relationships are the name of the game. "Honestly, we've only scratched the surface of the ecological interactions that are happening in a landscape like my family's farm," Guzman says.

While corn, beans, and squash get most of the attention, a whole class of plants in Latin American polycultures goes unrecognized by mainstream US agriculture. Or when these plants are recognized, it's generally not in a flattering light. "These would be considered by Western standards a messy garden full of weeds," says Heidi Liere, the Seattle University agroecologist who conducts research with immigrant urban gardeners in California, "but they have a lot of biodiversity." The biodiversity provided by herbs, spices, medicinal plants—and also non-crop plants that are simply left alone—significantly boosts the ecological functioning of such agricultural landscapes, Liere is finding.

Steve Gliessman told me a story about his own reeducation on the matter of weeds when he first arrived at CSAT, the small Mexican college of tropical agriculture where the scientific field of agroecology was born. As a graduate student, Gliessman had focused on allelopathy—the capacity of plants to release compounds that either aid or inhibit other plants. He thought this would be a good subject for a participatory research project in the immediate vicinity of the college. In order to identify potentially allelopathic plants, Gliessman went around to farmers and asked them to list their most problematic weeds, assuming these plants would be likely to have the inhibitory properties he was looking for. But when he asked the question, farmers were puzzled. "We don't use that word, *maleza*," the farmers said to Gliessman, repeating the Spanish term for weeds that he'd formed his question around. "We call these plants *monte*." *Monte*, Gliessman explained to me, essentially meant "non-crop plant." Farmers would speak of *buen monte* or *mal monte*, but these weren't hard and fast categories, just passing descriptions of the current impact on their crops. "Sometimes the same plant could be both," Gliessman told me, chuckling.

Miguel Altieri, one of the other scientists who laid the early groundwork for agroecology, had a similar experience in Tlaxcala, where he conducted a study of corn production in the late 1980s with fellow entomologist Javier Trujillo. Tlaxcalan farmers didn't use the word *maleza* either, Altieri and Trujillo found, but spoke of the wild plants growing in and around their fields as *hierbas*, *arvenses*, or *quelites*. Used as food, medicine, and even roofing material, these "weeds" were central to Tlaxcalan agriculture, providing an important source of minerals and vitamins such as calcium, thiamine, riboflavin, vitamin A, and vitamin C.

Just as traditional Mesoamerican farmers have embraced non-crop plants, they have often expressed a similar attitude toward insects. Agroecologist Helda Morales learned a memorable lesson about this outlook on pests when she traveled through the mountains of her native Guatemala in the 1990s to conduct dissertation research with Mayan corn farmers. When she asked them about their pest problems, she got an answer much like the ones Steve Gliessman and Miguel Altieri got when they asked Mexican farmers about weeds. "We have no pest problems," the Mayan farmers told Morales. Reformulating her questionnaire, Morales began asking farmers to list the insects that lived in their milpa. She got lots of answers, including several species that were categorized as corn pests by her university colleagues. So she asked the farmers why these insects weren't a problem for them. Again, she got a flood of answers, as farmers described the intricate ecological interactions that kept insect populations in check. By maintaining such high levels of biodiversity, Morales found, these farmers were able to keep the ecosystem in balance, so that no one species could dominate.

The lab group Morales worked with as a graduate student, directed by John Vandermeer and Ivette Perfecto at the University of Michigan, has documented many such Indigenous biocontrol systems. Working on Mexican and Central American coffee farms, an adaptation of traditional Mayan forest farms, the Vandermeer-Perfecto lab has charted mind-bendingly complex pest control food webs. In one case, a farmer alerted the researchers that the arrival of migratory birds would take care of his pest insects. The researchers confirmed that this was indeed true. But not because the birds ate the insects. Rather, the insects were consumed by parasitic wasps. But the reason the wasps were around was that *their* predators, spiders, were consumed by the birds.

Even the soil fungi that Guzman studies are part of these complex webs. She's not directly studying this relationship (yet), but other researchers have correlated the presence of these fungi with "herbivore resistance"—plants' ability to fend off and recover from pests. As scientists are still working to fully understand, soil fungi stimulate vast communities of plants to release chemicals that attract natural enemy insects. Just as Olivia Watkins explained to me, the fungi connect underground networks of plant roots, allowing the plants to "warn" one another about the presence of herbivores as soon as one of their number gets nibbled on.

While immigrant farmers from Mexico and Central America may have varying knowledge of how ecological pest control works, researchers have found, they are more likely to use these methods than White farmers, who more commonly reach for chemical pesticides. It's partly an issue of money—nonwhite farmers often have less access to capital, and pesticides aren't free. But perhaps more important are the experiences that immigrant farmers have had as farmworkers on industrial farms, which rely heavily on these chemicals. Many have suffered health consequences as a result, or know others who have. They don't want to expose their own families, or leave residues on food that they plan to eat themselves. Indeed, some researchers have found the desire to get away from pesticides is often the main reason farmworkers leave their employer and start their own farm.

Getting out from under this oppressive system of farm labor and restructuring rhythms of work is key to Mesoamerican regenerative agriculture traditions, I learned from Guzman. While it has become something of an assumption in the US that farm labor will be unhealthy, unpleasant, underpaid, and unfit for all but the most marginalized members of society, this is not so everywhere.

## The Care of Living Matter

When Guzman first visited her family farm in Mexico as a nine-year-old girl, she arrived during the harvest. Over the course of her childhood in the Central Valley, Guzman had learned what to expect from harvest time. Long hours apart from her parents. The exhaustion on their faces when they came home, struggling to marshal the energy to play with her. That godawful smell of rotting vegetables on their clothes. But the harvest in El Pedregal was completely different. Whole families participated together, helping one another and their neighbors in a somewhat raucous ritual that made the long hours feel more like a party than a slog of a workday. Physical labor was interspersed with food, laughter, conversation, and music, as well as profound expressions of gratitude for the bounty of the earth—in which all those involved would share.

This, Guzman realized, is what farming looked like when it wasn't wage work for an oppressed few but an entire community's way of life.

Anthropologist Roberto Gonzalez witnessed something similar when he traveled to a remote village in Oaxaca, Mexico, to study the agricultural practices of the Zapotec people. Gonzalez's book about his experiences, *Zapotec Science*, mentions several of the things you might expect from an account of ecological agriculture, such as intercropping and the building of maize mounds. But not until page 167. Far more striking to Gonzalez was the way in which labor was organized in the Zapotec village where he lived for two years, which had no "working class." Rather, everyone was expected to contribute to the *mantenimiento* or "maintenance" of their household and community. Quoting census figures, Gonzalez noted that three-fourths of the region's "economically active" population were "farmers." And yet, he observed, farming was seldom referenced as a distinct activity or job by the villagers themselves. Instead, the work of *growing* food was understood as part of a much larger process that also included grinding corn, making tortillas, cooking, and, ultimately, eating. Villagers referred to this whole suite of activities as mantenimiento—crossing over the boundaries drawn by English-language distinctions between production and consumption, work and leisure.

As a result, Gonzalez found, physical work was not considered unpleasant or undesirable, but simply a normal part of everyday life. Villagers designed ergonomic tools fitted to their users' bodies and organized large tasks like sugarcane grinding as festive group activities, accompanied by music, socializing, and feasting. With agriculture—or rather mantenimiento—so thoroughly woven into the fabric of community life, staple food crops were naturally seen as community members themselves, cared for according to the same norms of reciprocity that governed interpersonal interaction. This level of care for food and people was possible because all villagers were so intimately familiar with the life cycle and ecology of these plants, having worked directly with them since their early childhood years.

Given that everyone in the Zapotec village was so familiar with how to utilize the food and other resources, Gonzalez noted, virtually nothing was wasted, and environmental problems could be corrected quickly. And perhaps because there was no urgent need to escape work, the local concept of development or *desarollo* referenced the cyclical processes of the seasons, plant growth, and the human life cycle, rather than any sort of accumulation or transcendence of one's lot in life. "Zapotec farming," Gonzalez concluded, "appears to be a scientific and technological system in which the care of living matter—broadly construed as humans, animals, plants, earth, and water—is a means of achieving *mantenimiento* or maintenance of individuals, families, villages, and village lands." Gonzalez's book gets at perhaps the deepest layer of Mesoamerican regenerative farming traditions—which is also what is so often lacking in these farmers' immigrant experience. Guzman and the other researchers I spoke with struggled to put words to this quality, but it centered on the idea of "home."

In the dominant US context, making a home typically means eradicating other species. This is why conservation groups are so concerned about development. More houses mean less wildlife. And yet this isn't a necessary correlation. The tropical forest of the Maya lowlands is a richly biodiverse ecosystem, teeming with rare and endemic species. But it's also very much a human creation—managed for generations with fire and other tools to create an ecosystem in which more than 95 percent of the dominant tree species have utility for humans. For Mayan people, making a home for themselves has also meant making a home for their fellow species, including those that pollinate their crops, eat their pests, and enrich their soil.

Meanwhile, for Mexican and Central American immigrants struggling for a foothold in the US, making a place for themselves is often synonymous with creating a sanctuary for plants, insects, and even the microscopic soil organisms that Guzman studies. If we're willing to learn it, here is a profound lesson about how humans can be a beneficial participant in ecosystems, just like those soil fungi.

Guzman's childhood memories are mostly of small spaces: the trailers where she stayed with recently arrived relatives, the warehouses where she visited others. Her own family shuffled between various government housing developments before landing semipermanently in a home of their own. But even in these temporary and seemingly impossible spaces, many of Guzman's family members found a way to surround themselves with flowers, familiar foods, and plant medicines. "People can't bring their houses with them when they cross the border, they can't bring their family," Guzman explains, "but they can bring their food and they can bring their recipes and they can bring their seeds."

Industrial agriculture has taken a toll on these once fertile grasslands, unleashing much of their stored carbon into the atmosphere. As a result, there's not much for soil organisms to eat, and many of the microbes that powered this formerly vast carbon sink are gone. Low in organic matter and often bare for much of the year, these valley soils now emit worrying quantities of the greenhouse gas nitrous oxide, the inevitable result of applying heavy doses of chemical fertilizer to a soil that has little biological buffer to take up the excess. Meanwhile, industrial dairies release methane into the atmosphere, adding to the valley's greenhouse gas footprint. But as the diverse seeds planted by immigrant farmers begin to sprout, life is being infused into this beleaguered valley. Selected over generations to thrive in harsh conditions, these plants are prepared for life in a warming world. Hardwired to find microbes in the soil, they are calling out (presumably through root exudates) for their partners, fungi. And somehow, despite all the years they've been left searching for roots to sustain themselves, the microscopic fungi are coming back. These tiny organisms offer a far-reaching hope—the hope of sucking carbon out of the atmosphere and reinfusing it into millions of acres of degraded soils just like these.

## "Emancipation Never Really Came to Agriculture"

And yet, while more people of Mexican and Central American heritage are becoming farm owners, the vast majority of agrarian immigrants from Latin America remain exploited laborers on industrial operations. Even after recent increases, farmers who identify as Latino own just 3 percent of US farms. Meanwhile, they constitute 83 percent of US field workers. The reason for this massive gap, researchers say, is simple. Built on plantation slavery, US agriculture has never evolved beyond its dependence on an oppressed workforce. "Emancipation," says Union of Concerned Scientists agronomist Ricardo Salvador, "never really came to agriculture."

In the US, both scholars and the public have long subscribed to the idea of the "agricultural ladder": the idea that "all individuals who work the land diligently with their own hands . . . have access to upward agrarian mobility." This national story about hardscrabble rural folk working their way to prosperity remains central to US culture and politics. But it is largely a myth. In reality, agrarian wealth in the US has mostly been built by unpaid or underpaid agricultural workers—whose centrality to the farm sector constitutes the very reason they could never be allowed to ascend the agricultural ladder. Technically, we no longer allow slavery. But for agribusiness to maintain its current profits while selling food so cheap, somebody still has to harvest the crop for meager wages. Somebody who's not in a position to complain.

As I'd learned from Olivia Watkins, slavery didn't really end after the Civil War. White plantation owners simply used sharecropping, Jim

Crow laws, and, if necessary, racial terror, to maintain de facto slavery and quash Black farm ownership. And as I learned from Guzman, exploitation didn't end when Black agricultural workers fled southern farms in the so-called Great Migration. Rather, their place in the US agricultural economy was largely taken up by immigrants from Mexico and Central America, who were oppressed in nearly all the same ways. Importing temporary migrant workers from south of the border became the new means for US agribusiness to exploit noncitizen workers.

Mexicans were first recruited as temporary laborers during World War I, on six-month visas. This arrangement was greatly expanded with the 1942 establishment of the Bracero Program, which would bring more than two million Mexicans to the United States to work in the fields. Bound to a specific employer, Braceros received wages (from the Mexican government) only once they completed their contract and returned home to Mexico. The temporary workers had no recourse for exploitative treatment and abuse, which was rampant. Yet two million Mexican laborers were not enough for US agribusiness, and growers began encouraging others—without papers—to migrate as well. The presence of large numbers of non-White people in predominantly White rural communities laid racial anxieties bare.

In 1954, the US government created the first federal program to explicitly target and deport Mexican immigrants. Termed "Operation Wetback," the initiative deported 1.3 million people, some of whom were legally working in the country as Braceros. At the same time, Operation Wetback led untold millions of immigrant farmworkers to retreat into the shadows—in the face of the first public relations campaign to brand Mexicans as "illegal." Growers, initially concerned that anti-Mexican hysteria might eliminate their labor force, discovered that "illegal" workers were even easier to exploit than temporary ones. And so it has gone, for over half a century: essential as laborers and unwelcome as citizens, Mexican immigrants and their polycultural farming traditions have been continually and systematically displaced.

If we want a more regenerative food system, we'll need to replace this approach to labor with something far less hierarchical—something more like mantenimiento. Farmworkers and aspiring farmers need more support to start their own farms or form cooperatives, so they can prioritize care for land and community and benefit from their own efforts. They need secure access to land, water, and equipment—resources that are currently locked up in the hands of a few. Meanwhile, workers of all sorts need more time and access to grow and cook some of their own food and participate in a vibrant community food culture that closes nutrient loops. The structure and conditions of work are seldom raised in discussions about how to store more carbon in soils, but the two issues are powerfully connected. In our current food system, the exploitation of people and the exploitation of land are inextricably joined together. Our future food system must be one of mutual flourishing.

When she gives presentations, Guzman begins with an image by artist Ricardo Levins Morales. The piece depicts an industrial coffee plantation, with large patches of bare earth between squatty, uniform bushes. But in the center of the image, a brown hand holds up a rendering of what the landscape *could* look like—a healthy forest with many different crops growing in a diverse mixture. "I really like it because it symbolizes my own research motivations," Guzman says. "I want to help create the landscapes that those brown hands imagine."

~

To create such a regenerative agriculture, we'll also need the help of another group of farmers whose story has been ignored and misunderstood for decades. Before the US began recruiting the majority of its agricultural labor force from Central America, waves of immigrants from a different continent also attempted to ascend the fabled "agricultural ladder." These immigrants came with regenerative traditions as well: indeed, their masterful closed-loop strategies for recycling nutrients were the inspiration for the organic movement. But they too were systematically prevented from gaining a foothold in US soil. Historically banned from immigrating, barred from owning land, and even incarcerated due to unsubstantiated fears of disloyalty, these immigrants have nonetheless begun to reclaim their place in both this country's agrarian past and its agrarian future.

# CHAPTER 4
# Putting Down Roots

When Aidee Guzman was still scouting for collaborators, she got a tip about a monoculture squash farm just outside of Fresno. Excited, Guzman and her research assistant drove off toward the intersection they'd been directed to, hopeful the farmer might give them permission to take some soil samples. The mood in the car was light and jocular, but in the back of her mind, Guzman was doing math. Silently tabulating the farms she'd recruited so far, she couldn't help but worry about how many more she still needed.

In order to make statistically sound comparisons, Guzman had a daunting task. She had to find at least thirty small farms that grew one of her "focal" crops—squash or eggplant. Half of these farms needed to be monocultures, half needed to be polycultures, and in all other ways, the farms had to be reasonably comparable—so that confounding variables wouldn't invalidate her findings. For months, Guzman had been poring over satellite maps and driving around Fresno, confident these farms existed even though some of her senior colleagues were concerned that she might be attempting the impossible. After all, no one had ever successfully completed a study like this before.

When Guzman and her research assistant arrived at the corner they'd been directed to, they pulled over and scanned the landscape. Squash was nowhere in sight. Instead, they found themselves at the back of what appeared to be the most diverse farm they'd seen yet: rows upon rows of nearly every crop Guzman knew, as well as several she didn't recognize. From a distance, Guzman began enumerating the familiar plants: lettuce rows here, a small peach orchard there. Curious, she and her research assistant got out of the car and walked closer.

Still half hoping to eventually find squash, Guzman's eyes were drawn to a row of trellises. Hanging from the nearest trellis was a spiky, dark green gourd, sort of like a cross between a zucchini and a porcupine. This striking fruit was in the squash family, all right, but it was nothing like the plants Guzman's family grew in their gardens. Guzman scanned her memory for the name of the plant, knowing she'd seen it before. Just as she remembered—bitter melon!—a sprightly Asian woman with neat bangs popped out from behind a row of plants. "Hello," the woman said, "can I help you?"

More than a little apologetic, Guzman and her research assistant explained that they were doing a study on soil health and that they'd been told there was a squash farm in the area. To their relief, the woman smiled. "Ah yes," she said, "two farms over that way."

As she absorbed the directions, Guzman was struck by the commanding presence of this slight farmer, who was no taller than she and clearly many decades older. As the daughter of two farmworkers, Guzman had seen women on Central Valley farms all her life, picking crops and pulling weeds. This woman had clearly done both of those things for years, as evidenced by the calluses on her hands and the dirt under her fingernails. But something about the way she held herself, chatting comfortably in her second language, suggested that she wasn't working on someone else's farm. This place was hers.

Guzman was already halfway to the squash farm when the obvious dawned on her. "Sorry to bother you again," she said when she eventually circled back to the woman who'd given her directions, "but would you be willing to participate in our study?" The woman happily agreed, introducing herself as Keu ("Koo") Yang Moua. The farm that Guzman serendipitously stumbled upon would turn out to have the highest diversity of beneficial fungi she'd seen yet.

## From Laos to Fresno

Well before the US officially entered the war in Vietnam in the 1960s, the Central Intelligence Agency began waging an all-out battle to defeat communism in Southeast Asia. As part of the CIA's secret mission, members of an ethnic minority group in Laos were recruited to fight alongside US military and special forces. These people, the Hmong, lived in remote mountain areas and practiced subsistence agriculture. They had no intention of leaving their villages. But when the US lost the war, the Hmong found themselves in mortal danger. Deemed political refugees by the United Nations, they began resettling in the United States, arriving in waves over the course of more than twenty years. Large numbers of Hmong settled in Wisconsin and Minnesota, assisted by resettlement agencies and the US government. Thousands more came to California, many of whom eventually landed in Fresno.

California's Central Valley—flat, dry, and frequently smoggy—was nothing like the humid tropical mountains the Hmong had farmed for generations. But since farming was what they knew, numerous Hmong families resolved to transplant their agricultural traditions to this strange new place. By 2008, a University of California survey identified 1,500 Southeast Asian farms in Fresno County, nearly half of them less than five acres in size.

The Yang family was among the first waves of Hmong to migrate to Fresno: after a stopover in a Thai refugee camp, they settled in the valley in 1976. Shortly after the Yangs arrived, daughter Keu married into the Moua family, raising five children. Though her husband had a good job, money was still tight. So in 1990, at the age of thirty-five, Keu Yang Moua leased an acre of land to try her hand at farming. "I tried to learn from the old people," Moua recalls. "The old people that farmed in Laos before they moved to Fresno." Moua leased two acres the following year, then three, then four. Eventually, she had built such a successful farm that her husband decided to quit his job: he could make more money farming with her.

When I asked Moua how many crops she grows, she laughed. "A lot," she said, before launching into a seasonal inventory. "Right now, the summertime, I've got a lot of tomato, bell pepper, eggplant. Winter-time, a lot of bok choy, spinach, lettuce, sweet pea, arugula, radish, red onion, garlic." Moua went on to list her tree crops: Asian pear, peach, orange, persimmon, jujube, and mandelo (or "cocktail grapefruit"). "You know moringa?" she asked. "I grow that too. And gai lan [Chinese broccoli], kohlrabi, brussels sprouts, carrots, daikon, okra, long bean, green bean, bitter melon, cucumber, Japanese cucumber. . . . Too many," Moua said, laughing. "I'm just an old lady."

Having a wide variety of crops is essential, Moua explains, because she sells her produce at a farmers' market. "At the farmers' market, it's a lot of people," she says. "Vietnamese, Chinese, Filipino, Cambodian, Mexican, Russian, Armenian . . . all these people, they have their own veggies." Moua has regular customers who come each week to visit her stall at San Francisco's oldest outdoor produce market, counting on her to be there with their favorite vegetables. So every Saturday she rises in the wee hours to make the two-hundred-mile drive, just as she has for some thirty years.

"I'm old now, but I still like to do my own job," says Moua, now in her sixties. "Lift the box into the truck, go to farmers' market, lift the box out of the truck. . . . Like the people exercise," she says, giggling, "that's what I'm doing."

In the few decades since they began resettling in the United States, Hmong farmers like Moua have become fixtures at farmers' markets, where they make up more than 50 percent of the vendors in some cities. In the upper Midwest, where small family farms gradually gave way to industrial corn and soy over the course of the twentieth century, Hmong farmers brought fresh vegetables back into communities that had all but lost their local food supply. And in California, they carved out a niche providing cultural foods to diverse immigrant communities in cities like Los Angeles, Sacramento, and San Francisco.

"It's not just Southeast Asian consumers," says Ruth Dahlquist-Willard, a University of California farm advisor who works closely with Hmong farmers in Fresno. Hmong farmers do grow an astoundingly diverse menu of crops for their own families and Hmong customers, she says, as well as for shoppers at farmers' markets throughout the state. But urban immigrant communities from across the Asian continent also rely on Hmong farmers, Dahlquist-Willard says, and as a result, these farmers have adopted a wide variety of other Asian crops. "I think some of those communities have gone up to Hmong farmers at farmers' markets and said, hey, do you know what this is and can you grow it?"

But the diversity of crops on Hmong farms isn't simply about meeting customer demand, Dahlquist-Willard adds. "The reason those farms are highly diversified is that they sell to farmers' markets that ask them to be diversified, but that also fits really well with the traditional practices and the crop rotation which that community has historically done back in Laos."

**Translating Traditions**

Before the "American wars" in Southeast Asia, Hmong farmers practiced what scientists refer to as "rotational swidden agriculture." The steep slopes of their tropical homelands were too fragile to farm continuously, so families rotated through a series of different plots, letting the land rest between crop cycles and using fire as a tool of regeneration—much like the Indigenous prairie peoples of North America. Because most Hmong lived far away from market centers, specialization and mono-culture weren't options. Families needed to grow a complete diet on their rotational plots, from staples like rice and cassava to vegetables, herbs, and even spices. The Hmong managed this diverse array of crops by taking turns working one another's farms. During peak harvest, groups of ten to fifteen people—typically extended family members—would all converge on a single farm. When they finished the harvest, they'd move on to the next place, then the next. As each crop matured, the crew was ready to efficiently gather the perishable produce when it reached its fleeting peak.

When the Hmong attempted to bring their reciprocal labor practices to the United States, however, they ran into a problem. According to California law, all workers on a farm—paid or not—had to be cov-ered by workers' compensation insurance, which could cost a small-scale Hmong farm up to $445 per year. Minimum wage law offered an exception for immediate family, but this was defined as nuclear fam-ily members, excluding the extended family members that had been part of Hmong households and labor-sharing norms for generations. When regulators began conducting multiagency labor law sweeps in Fresno County in 2004, Hmong farmers were confused and terrified. Officials descended on their farms without translators, fining them up to $25,000—more than many farmers earned in an entire year—for infractions they often didn't understand. Though the agencies insisted they were not singling out Hmong farms, University of California researchers investigating the incidents concluded otherwise, stating that the number of Southeast Asian farmers targeted by the sweeps "seems disproportionately high."

"[Hmong] farms are typically so small that the vast majority of them are not even captured by the U.S. Census of Agriculture," the researchers wrote. "Yet they are subject to many of the same agricultural regulations as are their corporate counterparts with vastly different historical circumstances." In the wake of the sweeps, at least fifty Hmong farms shut down for fear of being fined, and powerful seeds of mistrust were sown. That wariness had far-reaching consequences, the researchers observed, compounding the existing economic, linguistic, and cultural barriers faced by Southeast Asian refugees. Because they specialized in low-input farming techniques, Hmong farmers were strong candidates for organic certification, which could potentially mean access to California's top-dollar organic market. But certification required paying a fee, filling out paperwork (in English), and adopting new recordkeeping systems (also in English). To have any hope of jumping through all these hoops, Hmong farmers would need help from technical assistance providers—government officials they had come to see as enemies rather than potential sources of support.

To rebuild trust, agencies like the University of California Cooperative Extension service and the Natural Resources Conservation Service (NRCS) turned to Hmong employees. One farm at a time, these Hmong agents tried to help community members translate their traditional practices so that farmers not only complied with regulations but could get paid for their ecological management.

"In the old days, in the old country, they farm for a couple years, then they abandon it for a couple years," says Sam Vang, a Hmong soil conservationist with the Natural Resources Conservation Service in Fresno. "When they abandon it, they allow the vegetation to grow again, which makes sense back in that country—it's on a slope, high rainfall, so most topsoil is going to move down if you farm too long." Many Hmong farmers in the US still retain this concept of fallowing land to regenerate it, Vang found, so he decided they might as well earn money for their efforts to build the soil. "I say, that's fine if you want to do that," Vang says, "and at NRCS we call that 'conservation cover.'"

## Two-Thousand-Year-Old Innovations

As dozens of farmers streamed into Keu Moua's place on an October morning in 2018, Sam Vang looked up at the sky and smiled. After a long summer of triple-digit temperatures and wildfire smoke, the air had cleared and the mercury sat at a benevolent sixty degrees: a great day to showcase Moua's conservation cover and the other soil health practices she and Vang had implemented on her farm over the past five years. "I always use her farm as a model," Vang told me. "You walk into her farm, right away you can tell: this is a farmer who can make a living."

By the time the program began at nine o'clock in the morning, some fifty people had arrived. Hmong women wearing visors chatted with husbands in baseball caps. Recently settled Syrian refugees gathered under a pop-up tent, taking seats next to longtime Punjabi farmers. A Sikh man in a checkered shirt and a turban grabbed a folding chair in the front, eyeing Vang's posters of Moua's cover crop. Supersized images of the thick, intensely green strip of vegetation filled a two-by-three-foot poster board, attracting farmers' attention. Labels in Hmong and English identified the plants Moua had used—vetch, bell beans, peas, and oats—as well as the dates of the photos, which had been taken months earlier in February and March.

Few immigrant farmers in the Central Valley can afford to take land out of production during the summer growing season, Vang explained. So he encourages growers to sneak in the soil-building cover *before* they start planting their crops: in the winter. The timing creates a challenge for Vang's demonstration-style pedagogy, though. "I can show them a beautiful cover crop in February, but are they going to remember it by the time they need to seed their own the next December?" Vang says. The best way to create a hint of February in October, Vang has found, are the enlarged photos, which are palpable enough to give farmers a sense of what they might plant on their own land. "Then we can walk around and show them the results," Vang said.

It's not hard to see the impact of cover crops on Keu Moua's farm, Vang told me, since she has rotated her soil-building crop around different sections of her land each winter. In addition to building up soil fertility, Moua's cover crop has significantly suppressed weeds—so much so that she has added cover crops to the understory of her orchard as well. Moua was eager to demonstrate the difference between two peanut crops, one that followed a cover crop, and one that did not. "The one where you have a cover crop, the plant's more healthy, more green, they have more peanuts in the ground," she said.

Another hot topic at the field day was compost, which has particular significance for Asian produce farmers in the Central Valley. Their soils are too sandy to support ginger, a key crop for many of their customers. But if they amend the land with compost, they can add enough organic matter to shift the soil texture—and ginger can thrive. To make the point, a farmer presenting at the field day held up two pieces of ginger—one grown with compost and one without. The size difference was striking enough, but the farmer went further, taking a bite out of each. It wasn't hard to tell which was tastier.

For many farmers at the field day, seeing cover crops and compost in action was a novel experience. These biological soil-building strategies are rare in the Central Valley, where decades of industrial agriculture have reduced organic matter to extremely low levels. Soils under such intense cultivation have become so degraded, says soil scientist Asmeret Asefew Berhe, that they can cause a chain reaction of water pollution that extends well beyond the farm. Meanwhile, farmers have to import nearly all the nutrients necessary for plants to grow. "One of my colleagues refers to the soils in the Central Valley as basically hydroponics at this point," says Berhe, who spent more than a decade of her career just an hour up the road from Moua's farm, as a professor at UC Merced. "You pump them with enough water and nutrients, you can grow a crop anywhere."

Aware that ecological farming approaches are uncommon in these parts, Sam Vang had billed the event at Moua's farm as an "innovation farming workshop," hoping to convince farmers that the atypical practices on display were forward-thinking glimpses of the future. Considering the past fifty years of advice given to farmers by the agency Vang works for, the United States Department of Agriculture, it was an apt characterization. As the USDA has gradually warmed to agroecological methods—driven largely by farmers' interest in trying something other than chemicals that run up their debt—cover crops and compost are indeed new innovations.

But given the predominantly Asian crowd at the field day, the word "innovation" was a little ironic. After all, the Asian continent is where the US organic movement got the idea to use compost and cover crops. As early organic reformers astutely noted, soil-building strategies like these have sustained farming regions from India to Japan for many thousands of years.

## "An Almost Religious Fidelity"

When University of Wisconsin soil physicist Franklin Hiram King took a nine-month tour of Asian farms in 1909, he was struck by the absence of mineral fertilizers, which most of his university colleagues considered essential. Instead, King observed, the farmers he met in China, Japan, and Korea "returned to their fields every form of waste which can replace plant food removed by the crops" with an "almost religious

fidelity." Impressed by the intricate systems of crop rotation and composting, King encouraged US farmers to follow suit. "These nations,"
King wrote in his classic book *Farmers of Forty Centuries*, "have demonstrated a grasp of essentials and of fundamental principles which may
well cause western nations to pause and reflect."

But the farming strategy that most captivated King was a form of
cover cropping he witnessed in rice paddies: a living mulch. Once rice
plants were well established, farmers would sprinkle seeds right into
their crop, seeds that would mature after the harvest into a vibrant
stand of Chinese milk vetch. Just before the vetch flowered, the farmers would cut the nitrogen-rich cover crop and compost it offsite, later
adding it back to the field just when the next rice crop needed a little
fertilizer. Fertility wasn't the only benefit of this living mulch, though.
The Chinese milk vetch also suppressed weeds, not only by shading
them out but also by releasing allelopathic chemicals to inhibit their
growth—just like squash in a milpa.

The English common name of the plant is apt, as the living mulch
was used widely in China, home to the earliest recorded use of cover
crops. In 500 BC, before vetch became popular, writer Chia Szu Hsieh
recommended mung beans as an ideal soil builder—with sesame as a
reasonable second choice. "Their fertilizing value," Hsieh crowed, "is
as good as silk worm excrement and well-rotted manure." Hsieh's comparisons give a good indication of the Chinese approach to agricultural
fertility at the time, which did indeed return biological materials to
farm fields with "almost religious fidelity," to use King's turn of phrase.
But even King's wording misses the mark, influenced no doubt by his
attempt to translate what he saw for the twentieth-century American
public. As Hsieh's 500 BC prose makes clear, Chinese farmers of the
time did not see manure and rotting plants as waste. They saw them as
a precious resource.

In the Lake Tai region, located in the Yangtze River Delta, farmers raised pigs specifically for their manure, utilizing the animals to transform their kitchen scraps into fertilizer. Human waste was composted and applied to the fields too, truly closing the nutrient loop. Grain crops were rotated with legumes, scavenging any nutrients that remained in the fields after the nitrogen-rich beans. Mulberry leaves were used to feed silkworms, silkworm excrement to feed pond-raised fish. "Traditional agriculture in China," writes agroecologist Luo Shilling, "used to be a system without waste."

It wasn't long before Chinese farmers learned to design agricultural systems that not only functioned on recycled nutrients but actually cycled the nutrients themselves. About 1,200 years ago, Chinese farmers started raising fish in rice fields, a practice that continues to this day. In such "co-cultures," fish poop can immediately be used as plant food. Moreover, the fish have learned that shaking the rice plants often rewards them with tasty insects, and they shake off about a third of pesky planthoppers in the process. Omnivorous, the fish also eat weeds—and chemicals released from their skin help inhibit diseases like rice sheath blight.

Following their success with fish, Chinese farmers began raising ducks in their rice fields as well. The birds were a bit more unwieldy, but also enriched the soil while reducing weeds and pests. Curiously, Chinese scientists have found, the gentle kick of duck feet stimulates rice plants to grow shorter and tougher, so they're less likely to fall down, or "lodge."

Although raising ducks in rice fields didn't take off everywhere, compost, cover crops, and crop rotation were widespread across the Asian continent for centuries. Closed-loop farming systems like those observed by King were commonplace in Japan, Korea, and India well into the 1900s, just as rotational swidden agriculture endured in Southeast Asia. Not until Norman Borlaug's Green Revolution came to the continent—in the form of subsidized fertilizer and crops that relied on it—did farmers begin to change course. Indeed, as the industrial methods promoted by Borlaug began to undermine even US agriculture, it was Indian peasant practices that struggling American farmers looked to for an alternative.

## Organic: A Movement with Asian Roots

In the early twentieth century, not long after Franklin Hiram King's trip to East Asia, the British government sent botanist Sir Albert Howard to India, which was then a British colony. Howard, the first director of the subcontinent's new Institute of Plant Industry, was instructed to teach modern scientific techniques to Indian farmers, presumably so the crown could collect more in taxes. Instead of teaching, however, Howard and his wife, Gabrielle Matthaei—also a botanist—found themselves learning. Like King, Howard and Matthaei were struck by the high level of fertility on the farms they visited, farms with no history of applying either chemicals or minerals. The duo carefully observed the farmers' practices, documenting what they saw. "By 1910," Howard wrote, "I had learned how to grow healthy crops, practically free from disease, without the slightest help from . . . All the . . . Expensive paraphernalia of the modern experiment Station."

Howard was particularly taken with the Indian farmers' system of composting, which he wrote up in English as the "Indore Composting Process." The process—and the philosophy behind it—would form the core of Howard's *An Agricultural Testament* and *The Soil and Health*— books that strongly influenced the organic farming movements in both England and the US. To this day, organic farmers cite Howard's famous Law of Return, declaring that all living matter that leaves the soil must somehow be put back. And they still compost in much the same way as Howard learned to do from Indian farmers.

Recycling organic matter back into the soil, as so many Asian farming systems were systematically designed to do, was for centuries the sole means of sustaining the fertility necessary to raise crops. There was simply no other way to supply plants with nutrients. But in 1909, while Franklin Hiram King was touring through China and Japan, a German scientist named Fritz Haber successfully demonstrated a process for synthesizing nitrogen. Instead of hauling manure around or procuring expensive minerals, farmers could now fertilize their crops with a jug of ammonium nitrate. Over the next few decades, synthetic fertilizer would become the darling of researchers, government officials, and of course chemical companies, which would earn windfall profits from selling their wares to farmers.

But much like Tuskegee professor George Washington Carver had done before him, Sir Albert Howard questioned whether commercial fertilizer was the equal of compost. While the two materials might be equivalent from a chemical standpoint, Howard argued, there was also a *biological* component to fertility. It was years before scientists like Aidee Guzman would unlock the secrets of tiny soil microbes, but with the help of Indian farmers who insisted their soils were alive, Howard had already caught a glimpse. To have truly healthy plants, he argued, you needed a *living* soil teeming with healthy critters that could not survive on fertilizer alone. They needed time-tested forms of sustenance: compost, mulch, or manure.

For Howard and the organic movement that followed him, replicating Asian farmers' methods of recycling organic matter was initially about soil fertility. This preoccupation was understandable; in the early twentieth century, soil conservation was a landmark environmental issue in both England and the US. Poor soils were widely seen as a dire threat to global food security and the survival of the human species.

But by the end of the century, the practices long maintained by Asian farmers would gain renewed attention in light of a new existential crisis: climate change.

With their commitment to recycling nutrients, Asian farmers did more than sustain farm fertility for some forty centuries. Their meticulously crafted, closed-loop systems also kept a lid on greenhouse gas emissions. Because nutrients were continuously being taken up and used by plants, they were far less likely to escape to the atmosphere as carbon dioxide, nitrous oxide, or methane. Meanwhile, cover crops and living mulches actually pulled carbon out of the atmosphere and stored it underground. Farmers would use some of this stored organic matter for future crops, but this too would eventually be recycled, as even human waste was returned to the soil. Meanwhile, a fraction of the carbon sequestered by cover crops would be routed deep into the soil profile, where it might stay for centuries. A synthesis of recent research estimates that even with current intensive agricultural practices, widespread cover cropping could store enough carbon to offset 8 percent of the direct annual greenhouse gas emissions from farming.

Using biological nitrogen also meant that traditional Asian farming systems weren't burning fossil fuels to make fertilizer, as industrial agriculture does today. Overuse of this synthetic fertilizer contributes to climate change not once but twice: generating emissions when it's manufactured and escaping from farm fields as nitrous oxide. This is one of the main reasons organic farmers lobbied hard for a certification system that disallows synthetic nitrogen, turning to strategies more like those long used in China, India, and Japan. Admiration for the farming systems developed in Asia is palpable in King's and Howard's writings, which largely give credit where it is due. And yet, even as early organic reformers in the US were adopting Asian farming *practices*, the US government was pulling out all the stops to exclude Asian farmers.

## Asians Not Welcome

When Asian people first began arriving in significant numbers in the nineteenth century, US farmers welcomed the new immigrants—as workers. As the mining industry gradually declined, Chinese laborers who had come for the gold rush shifted to farm labor, helping build California's farm sector into the fastest growing agricultural economy in the country. By 1882, seven out of eight farmworkers in the state were Chinese. But by then, the US had spent a decade in economic depression, spurring widespread unemployment. Blaming Chinese immigrants for taking their jobs, rural Whites lobbied the federal government to pass its first discriminatory immigration law: the Chinese Exclusion Act of 1882. Though Chinese merchants and diplomats could still enter the United States, Chinese laborers were banned.

Or at least, they were banned on paper. In practice, many Chinese immigrants—with more than a little encouragement from their employers—found ways to continue working in agriculture, falsifying paperwork and exploiting loopholes in the law. But being illegal meant the Chinese were largely stuck at the bottom of the agricultural economy, forever working low-wage jobs for someone else.

While the Chinese Exclusion Act failed to completely eradicate the presence of Chinese farmworkers, it nonetheless slowed the flow of immigrant labor enough to concern California's increasingly industrial growers. To fill the gap, they looked to Japanese immigrants: by 1910, two-thirds of Japanese Americans working in California were employed in agriculture. Like the Chinese before them, Japanese workers were hired at the bottom of the wage scale—paid less than either Whites or Mexicans. But once established in an area, Japanese laborers used collective bargaining tactics to demand higher pay, threatening strikes when perishable crops were about to ripen. One contract negotiation at a time, these Japanese communities began to build wealth, pooling money to rent land and then buy it. As more and more Japanese farmers purchased land, they hired more and more Japanese laborers—at higher wages than their White counterparts. They managed to take a promise always meant to be false—the idea that immigrant farmworkers could move up the "agricultural ladder" to own their own farms—and actually give it some truth. By 1920, Japanese farmers were growing about a third of all produce in California.

Unwilling to cede their grip on power, White farmers fought back, lobbying the California state government to pass a series of "alien land laws." The first such law, passed in 1913, prohibited noncitizens from owning land—and limited lease terms to three years. Though the law didn't specifically single out Japanese Americans, they were its clear target, as they constituted the largest Asian immigrant group legally ineligible for citizenship at the time.

Undaunted, immigrant Japanese farmers bought land in the name of their US-born children. Land purchased in the name of minors had to be placed in the guardianship of an adult, so Japanese immigrants found sympathetic Whites or Hawaiian-born Japanese American citizens (who had immigrated many years earlier) willing to serve as trustees. White allies also signed on as members of "dummy corporations," pretending to be stockholders of land that was actually managed entirely by Japanese immigrants.

Attempting to close such loopholes, California amended its Alien Land Law in 1920. Noncitizen Japanese farmers were no longer allowed to lease land at all. Nor could they be members of corporations that held title to land—no matter how many White people were also stockholders in the company. Again, Japanese Americans and their allies thwarted the law, this time by formally designating Japanese farmers as employee "managers" of land they were, in fact, illegally leasing. So in 1923, California updated the law again, this time enumerating every verb that could possibly connote a relationship to land. Under the revised law, noncitizen Japanese were not allowed to "acquire, possess, enjoy, use, cultivate, occupy, [or] transfer real property." More than a dozen states passed similar laws, not only preventing Asian immigrants from holding land but forcing them off land they were already farming.

In late nineteenth- and early twentieth-century California, the story repeated itself with one Asian immigrant community after another: Chinese, Japanese, Filipino, Punjabi. They came as farmworkers. They hoped to become farmers. But they were systematically denied access to citizenship and land ownership, ensuring that agribusiness would always have access to a pool of legally insecure laborers. This was the model that would later be applied to Aidee Guzman's family and millions of other immigrant farmworkers.

Despite the fact that Hmong farmers came to the US legally—as refugees—they were nonetheless slotted into the same exclusionary social framework, which by the 1970s had been solidly woven into rural America's economic and cultural fabric. Although the US had long since updated the 1924 law that banned Asian immigration, farmers in places like Fresno hadn't quite relinquished that act's stated purpose, "to preserve the ideal of American homogeneity." Like other Asian immigrants before them, Hmong farmers faced the perception that they weren't American enough to be trusted. And much like the Japanese farmers of an earlier era, the Hmong struggled to overcome persistent fears that their collective work practices and communal economies would prove "unfair" competition to White-owned farms.

As Hmong farmers faced multiple forms of discrimination, they also had to negotiate the capital-intensive environment of California agriculture, one of the most heavily concentrated and industrialized farm sectors in the world. As a result, they mostly ended up farming on short-term leases, often renting land for just a single season. Farming without secure land tenure put the Hmong in a precarious position. It also made adopting regenerative methods—including their own long-standing traditions—almost impossible.

### "You Cannot Plant the Tree"

As the field day at Keu Moua's farm continued, Sam Vang moved on from cover crops and compost to showcase a much less common practice that Moua had recently implemented: hedgerows. Vang walked the crowd over to a double row of what looked like ornamental bushes, laid out along a drip irrigation line and surrounded by woodchip mulch. It wasn't just pretty landscaping, Vang explained, pointing to the almond orchard across the street.

One of the major issues in the Central Valley, Vang told me, is that small vegetable farms are often located right next to almond orchards, which are ubiquitous around Fresno. Standard management practices for almonds involve a lot of pesticides, Vang explained, and the nut harvest kicks up big clouds of dust. For Hmong farmers, whose specialty vegetables are sensitive to both chemicals and dust, this can mean losing large portions of their crop. Double-row hedgerows, Vang says, can help mitigate the problem. For the outer row, he recommends plants that can quickly grow to ten feet, providing a shield from dust and chemical drift. For the inner row, he suggests flowering plants that can host pollinators and other beneficial insects. Though Moua's hedgerow was just getting started when the field day guests came to check it out, she already had some of these insects buzzing around.

Ruth Dahlquist-Willard—the University of California farm advisor who's worked with hundreds of Hmong farmers in the Fresno area—led the portion of the field day focused on beneficial insects, sweeping her net through the nascent hedgerow. As Dahlquist-Willard collected insects from the hedgerow, she invited farmers to identify them on the Hmong-language guides she'd brought, pointing out which good bugs were helpful for controlling bad bugs. The insects made a good showing, and Dahlquist-Willard registered genuine interest among several farmers. But she also knew that hedgerows need time to establish: researchers estimate that the return on investment takes about seven years, minimum. And while Keu Moua has that kind of time, most Hmong farmers in the Central Valley do not.

Moua understands what it's like to farm on a short lease, because she used to do so herself. "Because you rent, you cannot plant the tree," Moua said, gesturing to her high-value perennial fruit crops and her hedgerow. "You have to do vegetables, only year by year." Many Hmong farmers would like to build up their soil so it can support a healthier crop, Moua told me, but they can't be sure they'll still be there to benefit when these kinds of long-term strategies start to pay off. That's why buying land, which the Mouas did in 2002, can be such a game changer. "She and her husband saved all the pennies they had and they put it into that land," Vang says of Moua. "She's always thinking about how can I take care of this land."

## Claiming a Place on American Soil

It's a sentiment that rings equally true for Nikiko Masumoto, who farms eighty acres of peaches, nectarines, apricots, and raisin grapes, just five miles south of the Moua place. Thirty-six-year-old Masumoto grew up on her family's orchard, where she was driving a tractor by age ten, but she never intended to stay. As a college student at UC Berkeley, the budding artist pursued interests in performance and social justice, earning acceptance to the master's program in performance as public practice at the University of Texas at Austin. Far from the conservative environment of the Central Valley, Masumoto nurtured pride in her Japanese American heritage and her identity as a queer woman. Urban audiences embraced her work, and she would eventually be invited to perform her one-woman show at the White House.

But as Masumoto dug deeper into Japanese American history for her master's thesis, she came to appreciate her ancestors' struggles in a new light. As she reflected on what it had meant for her grandparents to purchase their land—and for her father to stay—the connection between her family's struggle for belonging and the challenges she'd learned about in her environmental studies classes at Berkeley started to sink in. As she would later tell NBC News, "I came to realize one of the boldest, perhaps courageous things I could do with my life would be to come home and become the next generation to work the same farm."

The first Masumoto to immigrate to the United States was Nikiko's great-grandfather, Hizoko, who came to California in 1899. Her great-grandmother Tsuwa was next, arriving in 1918. The young couple logged long hours as farmworkers, picking crops and pruning grapevines up and down the Central Valley. Raising five children on laborers' wages, they dreamed of buying their own farm. But as California's Alien Land Law grew ever stricter, Tsuwa and Hizoko despaired of ever being able to purchase their own land. Their dream had become illegal. So they kept working other people's fields and saving up, hoping their children might one day be able to achieve what they could not. As the Masumotos' nest egg grew, the prospect of such a future seemed possible. And then came December 7, 1941.

In response to the bombing of Pearl Harbor, the United States government swiftly rounded up thousands of Japanese Americans—many of them citizens—and incarcerated them in internment (i.e., concentration) camps. Between 1942 and 1945, some 120,000 Japanese Americans were sent to remote, makeshift prisons across the West—for no reason other than their ancestry. The Masumotos were sent to the Gila River War Relocation Center, fifty miles south of Phoenix in the scorching Arizona desert. In this harsh environment, they were again tasked with farm work—this time to feed themselves. The incarcerated farmworkers relied heavily on daikon, or Japanese horseradish, since its spicy, starchy roots matured in less than two months. They found themselves eating it for every meal, even breakfast.

Twenty-year-old Takashi, the Masumotos' second-oldest son, was grateful for the farm work. As he would later tell his own son, it was "better than doing nothing." The energetic young Takashi, incarcerated just after his high school graduation, even signed up for a wartime emergency work program to harvest sugar beets in Montana. Anything, he said, just to get out of camp and off Block 23.

But there was one good thing about camp: Carole Sugimoto. The fifteen-year-old had grown up much like Takashi, working alongside her farmworker parents in the fields of the Central Valley. The whole Sugimoto family had been incarcerated after Carole's freshman year of high school, so the teenager had to earn her diploma at the only school she was allowed to attend: the improvised classroom at Gila River. For the Sugimotos, camp was particularly hard. Carole's father arrived at Gila River suffering from stomach cancer, then died within a month of the family's arrival.[56] Yet in the midst of tragedy, Carole found herself falling in love with a restless young man from Block 23.

When Japanese internees were finally released in the summer of 1945, life did not go back to normal. Families had lost homes, farms, businesses—three years of their lives. After serving in the army, Takashi Masumoto returned home to the Central Valley to find his parents—now fifty-three and seventy-three—living with four other families in an old grocery store, which they'd divided into rooms by hanging blankets. Determined to better their circumstances, Takashi found a barn for the three of them to live in and hustled farm work. He picked raisins. His mother joined a labor crew. His father pruned grapevines. Eventually, Takashi talked his way into a ranch management job with a tenant house, affording his family the dignity of running water and indoor plumbing.

In 1948, he married his sweetheart from camp, Carole Sugimoto. And in 1950, the family finally scraped together enough money to purchase a cheap forty acres, half of which was intransigent hardpan.

Determined to bring life to their little patch of earth, newlyweds Takashi and Carole gradually improved the soil. "My parents often used the Japanese term *bachi*, which roughly translates into 'what goes around comes around,'" their son would later recall. "I often heard 'take care of trees and vines and they'll take care of us.'" Beginning with grapes—some for drying into raisins and others for making cheap wine—the Masumotos eventually added peaches and nectarines to their growing farm, purchasing an additional forty acres in 1964. Their three kids helped with chores, and Taksahi's mom, Tsuwa, established a large garden where she grew food for the family's table: napa cabbage, Japanese eggplant, and even the daikon she'd once grown so sick of at Gila River.

With more opportunities than their parents could have ever dreamed of, the next generation of Masumotos looked to horizons beyond the farm. Takashi and Carole's daughter became a nurse in Los Angeles. Their eldest son became a computer scientist and invented a new circuit technology. Their younger son, David "Mas" Masumoto, went to UC Berkeley, majoring in sociology. As the increasingly industrialized agricultural sector squeezed out one family farm after the next, Takashi and Carole began preparing for the day when they'd retire their tractors and call it quits. But after graduating from college in 1976, Mas decided to come home for a while to help his dad. He never left.

## The Struggle for Connection

When I asked Nikiko Masumoto about how she builds soil health on her farm, she rattled off all the things her dad, Mas, implemented when he converted his folks' place to organic. He applied load after load of compost. He amended the soil with tons of manure. He planted cover crops too: red and strawberry clover, fava beans, and white vetch. All of these things, Mas learned, were practices his dad had once used as well, before he'd been encouraged to adopt synthetic fertilizers. The Masumotos were coming full circle.

"We do a lot of old-fashioned soil moisture testing too," Nikiko Masumoto told me, "as in, you get a shovel and dig, see what the top couple inches of soil look like. Is the color of the soil milk chocolate? Is it powdery white? Is it dark chocolate? I guess I like thinking about chocolate," she joked. But regenerative agriculture is about so much more than testing and amending soil, Masumoto stressed. "If we even just pause and think about the term regenerative," she says, "for me what jumps out is the idea of a generational connection. It's about a much deeper timeline of what it means to belong to a place."

Without that generational connection, much of the soil-building work on her family's land might never have happened, Masumoto says. When her dad decided to come back to the farm in the seventies, they planted trees her grandfather wouldn't have been able to tend on his own. And when she returned, three decades later, the horizon for investing in the land expanded again. "My dad says, as one farmer, you get forty harvests to study your land, to refine your craft," Masumoto says. "But when I came home, it doubled to eighty." There's no recipe for taking care of the land at her family's farm, Masumoto explained. Responding to the different needs of each season requires intimate memory of the place, an ability to read between the lines of a soil sample like you might parse the terse conversation of a taciturn family member rendered silent by trauma. "My dad just has years and years and years of notes of observations on the farm," she says.

For Masumoto, such long-term planning is essential for responding to climate change, which is already hitting hard in the Central Valley. Shortly after she returned to the farm, California entered a devastating drought—the worst in recorded history by many measures. In just two years of the five-year dry spell, California farmers lost $1.7 billion, with 72 percent of those losses impacting the southern Central Valley where the Masumotos live. As their neighbors scrambled to find more water to save their crops, the Masumotos did a curious thing. They shut some of the water off. "If extreme drought is part of the future of our farm," Nikiko Masumoto said, "we want to know what it looks like if we irrigate less, mimicking what it might be like if we have less access to water in the future."

In order to cut off the water earlier for some trees in their orchard, Masumoto and her dad built furrows to stop their irrigation from reaching the end of each row. At the end of the summer, they sized up the end-of-row trees to see which had sustained the most damage. Some of the water-starved trees were clearly suffering, but not all of them. In certain rows, the reduction in irrigation was "virtually unnoticeable." The trees that did the best were the Sun Crest peaches, an orchard Mas had planted with his dad when he was twelve. The fifty-year-old trees showed few signs of stress, despite the historic lack of water. "The canopy of roots must be so extensive and developed," Nikiko Masumoto postulates, "that it helped the trees adjust and withstand drought more than our younger orchards."

Hanging on to trees for half a century sounds "completely insane" to a conventional peach farmer, Masumoto told me. I confirmed her assessment on a neighboring peach farmer's blog, which explained that "Year 4 through 8 are peak production times . . . by about year 12 the production amount has lowered so much that it is beneficial to the grower to replant a new variety." It's true that the Sun Crest orchards don't produce the highest volume of fruit, Masumoto says. But the trees carry so much family history that her dad couldn't bear to cut them down. The "emotional wisdom" of that decision, she said, is hard to separate from the ecological resilience it has bestowed on her farm.

## Tackling Food Waste at Its Core

Shortly after Nikiko Masumoto was born, in the 1980s, the price for Sun Crest peaches plummeted. The Masumotos' fruit broker suggested they dump their Sun Crests: the box, Masumoto recounts, was worth more than the fruit. Mas refused, selling the twenty-pound boxes of peaches for fifty cents each. "We essentially paid people to eat our fruit that year," Nikiko Masumoto says, "because my dad could not bow to the waste mentality of that request."

The Masumotos' experience was no anomaly: waste has become one of the most pressing problems with the industrial food system. Project Drawdown, a global coalition of scientists researching climate solutions, estimates that approximately one-third of all food is wasted, accounting for roughly 8 percent of global greenhouse gas emissions. Food gets trashed all along the supply chain, rotting in fields when markets plummet and spoiling in transit when distribution and storage are inadequate. Even when food reaches its destination unscathed, it is frequently rejected by supermarkets for cosmetic deficiencies and sent to the landfill in large quantities by consumers and restaurants who simply buy or serve too much. As researchers have explained to me, we end up spending a third more energy, water, land, and fertilizer than we actually convert into food, all of which generates unnecessary emissions. Then, when the wasted food finally hits the landfill and decomposes, it generates methane—a greenhouse gas some twenty-eight times more potent than carbon dioxide. On the bright side, this problem of unused food represents a significant portion of humanity's climate footprint that could conceivably be reduced. Cutting back on the volume of wasted food, Project Drawdown's scientists estimate, could shave emissions by as much as ninety gigatons over the next thirty years—about six times as much as we might save by switching to electric cars.

Tackling food waste is most frequently discussed as a problem of logistics, a matter of plugging holes in distribution channels or properly aligning supply and demand. Over the past decade or so, an overwhelming number of startups have developed apps and software that allow people with excess food to connect to agencies that serve the hungry. Other tech-driven approaches to food waste include inexpensive refrigeration "bots" and technologies that extend the shelf life of produce. Nikiko Masumoto applauds such efforts, but she also thinks the food waste issue cuts deeper. She recalls how her grandmother saved boxes of used rubber bands and plastic forks, exclaiming *mottai nai*: don't be wasteful. This is why her dad couldn't throw out those peaches, she says. He respected them too much.

"In Japanese culture, there's a thing you say before you eat which comes from Japanese Buddhism," says Berkeley Food Institute director Nina Ichikawa, whose own Japanese American family struggled to hold on to their flower farm through the tribulations of alien land laws and incarceration during World War II. "*Itadakimasu*. It means I gratefully accept this food, but also, I acknowledge the laborers who grew it, I acknowledge the trees, I acknowledge the farm, thank you to everybody who brought it to me. You're supposed to go down the whole list in your mind of how it got to your plate."

A culture that understands food with this kind of reverence is less likely to waste it, Ichikawa believes. It simply becomes too valuable to throw away. "It's more efficient to teach people that the whole system is connected and that it's related to the core life force that made you," Ichikawa says, "rather than screaming at them, don't throw away something. You make the food higher quality from the beginning and every bit of it is important rather than making cheap shit food that you don't mind to throw in the garbage."

It's important to treat food waste as the systemic social problem it is, Masumoto agrees, rather than some kind of personal failing. As proud as she is of her dad's decision to save the Sun Crests, she understands why such actions aren't more common. "What are farmers supposed to do when the price of the market is less than the price it costs to harvest it?" she asks. For her part, Masumoto attempts to tackle waste on all three fronts: lobbying government to fix systemic problems, fostering reverence for the everyday miracles that give us food, and applying her grandmother's philosophy of *mottai nai* in her day-to-day operations. When she was growing up, Masumoto said, the family had a practice of donating any fruit that was not cosmetically approved for sale. But shortly after she came back to farm with her dad, they ran into a problem. "We had so much," she recalls with frustration, "that some of the organizations we donated to couldn't take any more fruit. We had this amazing tasting fruit and no place for it."

The surfeit of unmarketable fruit was yet another casualty of the drought, Masumoto explained. To conserve water, she had cut back on irrigating her family's Gold Dust peaches, reducing the flow some 20 to 30 percent. The result was actually quite tasty, she said, since the lack of water concentrated the peach flavor. But their buyers said the apricot-sized peach was too small. No one would want it. No more willing than her dad to throw away fruit she'd worked so hard to grow, Masumoto launched an #EatSmallFruit campaign on social media, reaching out to buyers willing to tell the story of the petite peaches. She also started a drive-through program to sell the fruit directly, which she dubbed the "O, U Fab! Club": Organic, Ugly, and Fabulous. The small fruits weren't just "seconds," Masumoto wanted her customers to understand, they were flavorful, ecologically raised treasures that happened to look different than corporate supermarkets have led us to expect. "Move over narrow definitions of beauty," she wrote to the club's members. It's time to "radicalize how we view the aesthetic value of food."

By highlighting everything this fruit is connected to—climate adaptation, queer pride, a family farm trying to save water for their neighbors—the Masumotos have built a community around the small and oddly shaped peaches. As I learned when I drove out to the farm to purchase one of the boxes myself, loyal customers travel for miles to pick up their fruit—even in the midst of a heat wave or a pandemic—posting recipes and photos of their creations on social media. Joining something like the O, U Fab! Club appeals to our hunger to be part of something larger, Masumoto believes, a fundamental human desire to be connected to where our food comes from. While this kind of know-your-farmer enthusiasm for local food might seem like par for the course in California, Masumoto explained, it wasn't like this when her dad was her age. Like everything else that made her family's farm possible, it had to be built from scratch.

## The Asian Origins of California Cuisine

When Mas Masumoto decided to convert his family's farm to organic and embrace older peach varieties like Sun Crest, he was essentially breaking up with his fruit broker. Warehouses weren't interested in juicy peaches—or juicy stories. They wanted newly developed peach varieties that ripened redder, with a longer shelf life. They wanted fruit that was chemically guaranteed to be blemish free. But many Japanese American consumers were more discerning, says Berkeley Food Institute director Nina Ichikawa. They demanded high-quality, fresh, local produce, and they were willing to go the extra mile to find it. To ensure a supply of such produce, two Japanese American men started small grocery stores in Berkeley, which would blossom into the iconic Berkeley Bowl and Monterey Market. These were the markets that gave Mas and his peaches a shot, transforming "old and ugly" to "heirloom and organic."

At the same time, it was Bill Fujimoto of Monterey Market who helped Chez Panisse chef Alice Waters build a new culinary movement around fresh produce, Ichikawa says, laying the groundwork for farm-to-table dining. Fujimoto's efforts built on the path-breaking success of another Japanese American family, the Kushis, who founded one of the country's first natural food markets. What we now call "California cuisine," Ichikawa says, has deep Asian American roots. And yet, despite the key role of Asian Americans in building these premium farm-to-table markets, few Asian American farmers actually have access to them. It's an irony that troubles Nikiko Masumoto, who doesn't want her farm to be the exception. Looking around Fresno, she sees recent Asian immigrants still facing the same struggles her ancestors did.

As a fruit grower, Masumoto has to buy her vegetables, many of which she purchases from local Hmong farmers like Keu Moua. None are certified organic. Several of her Hmong neighbors continue the same type of farming they did generations ago in Southeast Asia, Masumoto notes, growing a diverse mix of crops and using hand labor instead of chemical labor. Many of these farms would meet organic standards if they were assessed. But the structures that are set up to support sustainable and regenerative farming don't meet their needs. "Very few organizations have staff members that are Hmong, or speak Hmong, or have staff members in the Central Valley," Masumoto says.

Leaving the Hmong out of regenerative organic farming initiatives is not only unjust, Masumoto explains, but a huge missed opportunity. "So many Hmong farms are still small scale," she says, "and when we're talking about the management-intensive realities of a lot of regenerative agriculture practices, small scale becomes an asset." As US agriculture has become more concentrated and mechanized, Masumoto says, farm communities have lost the skills for working directly with plants and soil, recycling nutrients in the closed-loop systems that made the Asian continent such a source of inspiration for the organic movement. If our nation's farm sector is going to change course in time to meet the climate challenge, we'll need to look to farmers who still have those skills—like the Hmong. "We need those small farmers," Masumoto says. "We need the people who can walk the fields and observe things."

~

Ultimately, Masumoto believes, the future of regenerative agriculture hinges on whether the people needed to practice it are afforded stable access to land. The possibility of belonging to a place—of being intimately connected to lives beyond our own—is central to healing our soils and our climate, she says, and it's exactly what's been stolen from immigrants like Masumoto's ancestors. We often point the finger at farm policy for destroying our rural environment, she says, but immigration policy and racialized incarceration are to blame as well. With the government systematically separating families from one another, ripping people away from any connection to land, it's no wonder there's not more organic matter beneath the surface of rural America. People were never allowed to put down roots.

CONCLUSION

# Healing Grounds

The communities featured in this book—the Indigenous, Black, Latino, and Asian Americans who are often collectively referred to as people of color—make up nearly 40 percent of the US population. They also account for more than 60 percent of the current population of agricultural laborers and an even more significant share of the historical agrarian labor force. By the time you start trying to quantify how many hours of Indigenous labor went into building up the soils that supported the past two hundred years of European American agriculture—not to mention the food and sustenance Indigenous peoples provided to settlers when they arrived—it becomes readily apparent that the US food system is almost entirely built on the work of Black and Brown people.

And yet, people of color own just 2 percent of the agricultural land in this country. If you grew up learning, as I did, that economic opportunity in the US is based on the philosophy of John Locke—that one earns property by "[mixing] labor" with the soil—this statistic is more than a little disconcerting. It's arguably one of the deepest forms of hypocrisy undermining our democracy, on par with voter suppression and grossly disproportionate mass incarceration. What's more, the total land area held in trust for recognized Native American tribes—the original stewards of the entire continent—is more than sixteen times smaller than the US agricultural land base, and the majority of these Indigenous lands are actually leased to White farmers and ranchers. This stark inequality in agricultural land ownership is not only unjust, it's also holding back regenerative agricultural practices—techniques that are rooted in the ancestral traditions of these very communities of color—that we desperately need to combat climate change.

"Everything goes back to the land," says Stephanie Morningstar, co-coordinator of the Northeast Farmers of Color Land Trust. "If you want to heal—the planet, our communities, racism—it's going back to the land together." Morningstar, a close ally of the Black Farmer Fund who I met through Olivia Watkins, is well versed in the connection between land and climate: in her previous job, she was actually a climate change researcher. But while Morningstar's research helped her understand how current land management worsens climate imbalance, it was her journey to reckon with her own family's past that brought her to working on solutions.

### "It Always Ties Back to the Land"

In April 2010, Morningstar's mother went to the hospital with what she thought was pneumonia. While Morningstar sat with her mom in the emergency room, a doctor came in and broke the news that she had stage IV ovarian cancer. She was dead within a week. "It was really intense for my family to lose our matriarch," says Morningstar, who cites her mom as her fiercest advocate and the person who helped her develop a relationship with land. "It set me on a quest to basically avenge her death."

To understand her mother's death, Morningstar first needed to find out more about her grandfather. Raised in Ontario near the Six Nations of the Grand River territory, the Indigenous youth had been sent to a residential school far from his community. Just like the boarding schools in the United States, Canadian residential schools used brutal tactics to "kill the Indian in the child," ripping children from their families and inflicting violent punishments when they spoke their own language or begged to be sent home. When Morningstar's grandfather emerged, he carried with him the scars of that traumatic experience. He moved to the United States and raised his family in western New York State, never speaking of his homelands on the other side of the border. To protect his family from the violence he had experienced, Morningstar's grandfather discouraged them from identifying as Indigenous or connecting to their heritage. And having been violated by Western institutions, he passed down a deep fear of Western medicine.

"The way that manifested in my mom is that she avoided the doctors all the time," says Morningstar. "And yet we weren't close to a place where we could do traditional medicine and because of our disconnect from our culture, we weren't able to access that type of medicine." Haunted by the harsh lights of the ER and the condescending doctor who had tersely delivered the news of her mom's death sentence, Morningstar vowed to create places where people like her mom could heal.

In 2012, Morningstar went back to the Canadian reserve where her family comes from, Six Nations of the Grand River, and cofounded an integrative healing clinic with a Mohawk physician and a Cayuga medicine helper. (The Mohawk and Cayuga are part of the Six Nations, or Haudenosaunee Confederacy, whose homelands stretch across the contemporary border between the United States and Canada. Morningstar identifies as Mohawk.) As she connected more strongly to her culture, Morningstar began to look at health differently. It wasn't just about caring for individual human bodies, she realized. "Really it's that connection between the land and ourselves, that's where our health comes from," Morningstar says. "And it's reciprocal—we have responsibilities to land."

With the encouragement of her mentors at the clinic, Morningstar went back to school for ethnobotany. There, she became an advocate for an Indigenous-led approach that maintained botanical knowledge within a larger cultural context. While in school, she agreed to help build an Indigenous conflict resolution framework for the child welfare system in Ontario, Canada, which led her on a journey across Ontario, learning about customary practices for conflict resolution.

"Again, it was tied to land," Morningstar reflects. "Any system that we're connected to—legal systems, governance systems, child welfare systems, the health care system—if you want to understand how we relate to each other and the world around us, it always ties back to the land." Land, however, was precisely what Morningstar and many of her Indigenous colleagues did not have access to. Morningstar's grandparents had squatted on a rotating series of parcels to grow subsistence food for the family. She herself had begged landlords for a place to raise her medicinal herbs, eventually getting permission to farm a piece of land under a walnut tree. "You can't grow anything under a walnut tree," Morningstar says, exasperated. "Everybody knows that."

Morningstar got excited when she learned about a mountaintop property in Vermont, surrounded by lush eastern woodlands. The herbalist who owned the place was looking to pass it on to a new steward, and Morningstar began dreaming of making a life there. "And then I found out that a wealthy White herbalist with tons of access to resources and capital bought it, for something over $1.5 million," Morningstar recalls. "It completely cut me off from any sense that this could be a reality for me."

By this point, Morningstar had become an outspoken advocate for rematriation of land to Indigenous communities, and she was gaining recognition for her activism within the herbalism community. Here was a group, Morningstar reasoned, that expressed profound reverence for Indigenous traditions—and that also happened to have a lot of wealthy members who owned large tracts of land. If rematriation was going to happen anywhere, this seemed like a promising place to start. Morningstar was heartened when the new owner of the Vermont property came up to her at a conference, expressing her intention to return the land to its original Abenaki stewards. But to Morningstar's dismay, the woman's words were just an empty metaphor. "To me, to even speak those words is to make a contract with the universe," Morningstar said. "But nothing ever happened."

Morningstar continued practicing herbalism but also worked as a researcher at McMaster University in Hamilton, Ontario, where she collaborated on Indigenous-led research projects dedicated to answering community-driven questions regarding climate change. Then friends started sending her a job description: a newly formed land trust was advertising a leadership position. "People kept sending me this job description," Morningstar recalls, "and they're like, you need to apply for this. I'm thinking, it's in the States. I'm in Canada. I already have a job." Finally, on the day before the application was due, Morningstar opened the job ad. It was Halloween, just before All Souls' Day and Día de los Muertos, and Morningstar was thinking about her mother. "Her fantasy had always been to build something called Shulerville," Morningstar told me, explaining that her mother's maiden name was Shuler. "All it was, she just wanted a piece of land where she could build a small house and then I could build a small house, and my sisters could and my aunties could, we could all live together and communally garden and feed ourselves and make things together."

When Morningstar opened up the job ad, she zeroed in on the mission of the new organization, which called itself the Northeast Farmers of Color Land Trust. She read that the group had formed to advance permanent, secure land tenure for Black, Indigenous, Latino, and Asian farmers, to steward the land in "a sacred manner that honors our ancestors' dreams."

"As soon as I read that," Morningstar remembers, "I thought, that's Shulerville."

Morningstar submitted her application, and within weeks, the new co-coordinator of the Northeast Farmers of Color Land Trust was spending her days figuring out how to make good on that mission. She knew there were thousands of people like herself, carrying ancestral responsibilities that could help rebalance power while healing their communities, the soil, and the planet—if only she could help them get secure access to some of that 98 percent of US farmland still in White hands.

And yet, Morningstar reflects, the problem is deeper than White ownership. If we want to manage the US landscape in a way that brings balance back to our planet, we not only need to question the Euro-American monopoly on farmland ownership. We have to question the Euro-American idea that land should be owned in the first place.

## When Land Is Fungible

In 2018, a young attorney named Neil Thapar drove across the country, consulting *An Indigenous Peoples' History of the United States* as a sort of field guide. "It cracked something in the training that I got as an economics student in college," Thapar recalls, "where land is treated as just some factor of production, a piece of capital that's interchangeable. In economics, they taught us that one piece of land can be bought and sold in replacement for another piece, in the way that money or some other object can be."

Thapar had gone on from his economics degree at UCLA to earn a law degree at the UC Hastings College of the Law in San Francisco. After finishing his JD, he'd taken a job leading the Food and Farm program at the Sustainable Economies Law Center in Oakland, where he'd been working on strategies to gain land access for a wide range of clients. One day, Thapar was trying to help urban tenants access gardening space. The next, he was trying to help immigrant farmers navigate complex lease agreements. As he continually bumped up against the same barriers, Thapar became frustrated. "That's the backbone of our entire economic system is that land is something that can be traded and that is fungible," Thapar said. "And yet on that cross-country trip, reading that book, I saw how false that is. How unique each piece of land is. And the attention and care that is demanded of us because of that."

As Thapar was trying to figure out some way through these immense structural barriers, he got a call from his longtime friend Mai Nguyen. Nguyen, a farmer and activist whose day job also involved navigating hostile legal and bureaucratic systems to try to secure land access for farmers of color, was ready to try a new approach. The two made a pact to leave their jobs and start a new kind of land justice project: one that would honor land as a relation, not merely a piece of capital.

Like Thapar, Nguyen (who uses they/them pronouns) had come to land access work through a blend of formal training and personal experience. Born in San Diego to Vietnamese refugees, Nguyen studied climate science at UC Berkeley, which eventually led them to pursue a career in regenerative farming. Nguyen drew up a long-term farm plan, building on the ecological relationships among each element of the farming system. "I come from this background of climate research and being raised Buddhist," Nguyen says, "so I've always been taught to see the interconnections of the world and to think about community and the future."

But just one year into what was supposed to be a five-year term, Nguyen's landlord broke the lease. "Sustainability depends on planning for the long term," Nguyen explains, "and without land tenure you just cannot plan. You cannot implement your mushroom inoculation system that requires at least three years to break down carbon material into really rich soil organic matter." Nguyen went on to become a leader in California's local grain movement and something of a celebrity among bakers, cobbling together leases and raising a whopping twenty-five varieties of diverse, locally adapted grains. Farming without chemicals or irrigation, Nguyen avoided conventional tillage by using sheep for weed management and draft horses for broadcasting seed. Heralded as a regenerative farming success story, Nguyen knew the truth: in order to farm, they had to commute over eight hours to land that could be sold out from under them at any minute. It was not sustainable.

The good news for anybody working on farmland access, Nguyen and Thapar explained, is that a historic swath of the nation's agricultural land is likely to become available as older farmers age out of the profession. Some estimates suggest that some four hundred million acres—half of the total farmland in the US—could change hands in the next decade or so. But the bad news is that virtually none of these acres appear to be destined for futures as milpas or buffalo pastures or agroforests. They are not likely to fall into the hands of tree-conserving Black farmers like Olivia Watkins, prairie-restoring Indigenous communities like the Blackfeet Nation, or soil-building immigrant farmers like those with whom Aidee Guzman conducts research. In fact, quite a lot of land transfer has already happened in recent years, Nguyen and Thapar told me, and not in the direction of regeneration or equity. Instead, these land deals have led to concrete and consolidation.

Incredibly, just as scientists are clarifying the key role of agricultural lands in fighting climate change, those very lands are being paved over. According to the American Farmland Trust, 25.1 million acres of US agricultural land—nearly the size of the state of Ohio—were converted to developed uses between 1982 and 2015. The climate implications of this land transition are staggering: a 2012 University of California, Davis study that compared an acre of urban land to an acre of irrigated cropland found that the urban land generated seventy times as many greenhouse gas emissions.

Meanwhile, the agricultural lands that remain are being consolidated. When retiring farmers sell, parcels are frequently purchased by deep-pocketed institutional investors (like pension funds), which manage the lands as financial assets rather than ecological systems. Teachers Insurance and Annuity Association of America (TIAA), one of the largest pension fund managers in the country, now owns nearly two million acres of farmland, worth almost $6 billion. In the Mississippi Delta region alone, the pension giant owns nearly as much farmland as all the Black residents of the region combined.

So long as land retains a legal identity as a fungible piece of capital, Nguyen and Thapar believe, it will be nearly impossible to bid against giants like TIAA, whose interest in land is purely extractive. If regenerative agriculture is going to have any chance to scale out to the extent necessary to address our climate imbalance, we have to shift the way we relate to land.

## A Space for Un-Property

Morningstar walked me through the Northeast Farmers of Color Land Trust's approach to this work of reimagining land relations. The non-profit, Morningstar explained, is actually a hybrid of two different types of land trust. On the one hand, it operates as a community land trust, drawing on the model innovated in 1969 by Black farmers Shirley and Charles Sherrod when they created the New Communities collective farm in Albany, Georgia. At the same time, it also operates as a conservation land trust, drawing on a model ordinarily used to conserve wilderness but increasingly being applied to preserve the ecological integrity of agricultural lands as well. Given that community land trusts typically have a mission to expand access (usually to affordable housing in high-rent urban cities), while conservation land trusts typically aim to restrict it (in the interest of protecting nature), Morningstar has gotten some funny looks when she tells people that Northeast Farmers of Color Land Trust is a hybrid of the two. But that's exactly the point, she says. "Our understanding is that reconnecting people with land—particularly people of color—can be beneficial for both sides of that equation."

In the short term, the land trust negotiates equitable leases for farmers of color, vetting landowners to ensure that terms are fair and that the place and relationship provide a "safer space." Longer term, the trust aims to acquire at least two thousand acres of land, with the goal of providing affordable, long-term leases to some fifty farmers of color who commit to regenerative agriculture covenants. But the work isn't just about land acquisition, Morningstar explained. It's also about ensuring that farmers have the resources and training needed to succeed. In addition to connecting farmers with free technical assistance, the trust matches farmers with culturally appropriate business planning services and helps them access markets for their products. The trust also collaborates with "The Ecosystem"—a collective of five organizations dedicated to advancing the success of Black farmers, including the Black Farmer Fund, led by Olivia Watkins, and Soul Fire Farm, where Watkins once apprenticed and now sits on the board. Finally, the land trust uses its platform to advocate for climate justice and food sovereignty policy, pushing for reform to laws and public programs that have long discriminated against farmers of color and prevented them from accessing land.

Most importantly, Morningstar emphasizes, the land trust doesn't do anything without first consulting the Indigenous communities who are the original stewards of the land. Regardless of whether the US federal government has "recognized" a particular Indigenous community, they begin any discussion about land by reaching out to the traditional Indigenous governance bodies for that place. "My question to them is essentially, if we are going to be receiving a donation of land in your territory, what would you like us to do?" Morningstar explains. "Rematriation? A land tax? Do you want seeds stewarded on these lands?"

One of the primary tools Morningstar uses to work toward shared sovereignty is something called a "cultural respect easement," which stipulates specific forms of Indigenous access or Indigenous-informed management of land. As a hypothetical example of such an easement, Morningstar explained that a Vermont landowner in Abenaki territory might have a number of ash trees on their property. The Abenaki, who make traditional baskets using ash trees, might negotiate an easement with the landowner, who could agree to call a designated representative whenever an ash tree fell, so that the Abenaki could harvest it. Such easements could also grant access for hunting, harvesting, ceremony, reburial of ancestors, or simply be open to definition by the nation, Morningstar told me.

For Morningstar and her team, the ultimate goal is to bring all the threads of their work together into a several-hundred-acre community. This community would integrate all the functions of the land trust, with space for incubator farms, common areas for food production, childcare and health care services, and ongoing ecosystem restoration. Informed by shared sovereignty with Indigenous original stewards, the community would recognize the personhood of nonhuman beings, who would have explicit rights within its shared governance system.

As the co-coordinator of a land trust that both wants to acquire fee-simple titles and, ultimately, to abolish them, Morningstar finds herself in a complex position. "A land trust is meant for perpetuity," she explains, "so we need to be able to take our time and do it right if we want to ensure that this lasts forever." Then she pauses. "Or at least as long as the colonial system that supports a legal entity like a land trust," she clarifies. "We say land sovereignty when we talk about our work, but to be honest, land won't be sovereign until this system doesn't exist anymore."

Nguyen and Thapar confront a similar dilemma, as they aim to create an analogous network of communally managed land in California.

Suffering from land insecurity themselves and seeing the urgent need for farmers of color to attain secure land tenure, they have steadily gathered colleagues to mount a concerted effort to gain farmland. The pair have named their project Minnow, and they were initially reluctant to even characterize it as an organization or charter it as a nonprofit. "To have a pathway toward something different, we need to use the tools that are available to us in certain respects," Thapar explains, choosing the word *container* to describe what Minnow is. "But I also want us to be able to embody and provide a way in which we can use the tools available to us but also think beyond them."

Like Morningstar, Nguyen and Thapar have established a land acquisition fund to secure farmland. They are now designing "creative means" to enable land tenure for farmers of color and worker ownership of farm businesses, while furthering indigenous sovereignty and rematriation. They have begun building an Indigenous consultation process, and they are working with farmers of color to identify properties and fundamental infrastructure needs for their operations to be successful. No matter how much capital Minnow raises—and their goals are ambitious—they know they could never buy out the entire California farm sector. But that's okay, Thapar says, because the process they hope to catalyze starts in people's imaginations.

"My hope is that the concrete steps we take toward community control of land create more space for dialogue, so that we build from the collective wisdom that exists of alternative models of relating to land," Thapar says. Indigenous Californians have a wealth of such wisdom, he adds, as do many people whose ancestors built long-standing relationships with other lands that were subsequently colonized. Thapar cites his own family's experience of being assimilated into the US property system, having spent generations in India. In India, Thapar says, precolonial relationships to land have persisted, at least in pockets, so there are places where land isn't entirely a fungible commodity. "Even if you don't practice [these land relations] yourself, you think it's possible because it exists within your eyesight or at least you hear about it," Thapar says. "Whereas here [in the US] that's not the case for so many of us." By creating a few, interconnected oases of un-property, Nguyen and Thapar hope to foster confidence that a different way of relating to land is possible. Such confidence, they believe, could drive the public policy change needed to actually achieve that vision, so that regenerative farmers of color can apply their ancestral knowledge at the scale needed to make a dent in climate change.

There are signs this may be starting to happen. In early 2021, Congress approved Senator Raphael Warnock's bill to provide $4 billion in debt relief for farmers of color, plus an additional $1 billion to help these farmers acquire land and form cooperatives. As this book goes to press, Senator Cory Booker is still pressing Congress to pass his bill, which would grant up to 160 acres of land to both current and aspiring Black farmers. Many of the farmers of color who helped design these policies had experienced land reforms at a hyperlocal scale, through a collectively managed garden or farm led by members of their own communities. "Once it feels like something you can touch," Thapar remarks, "it feels more real."

## Healing Grounds

As I spoke with the trio of land justice advocates, I realized how fully my understanding of regenerative agriculture had shifted. In the beginning, I'd pored over research papers about carbon sequestration and soil organic matter, trying to pin down the potential for agricultural climate solutions in technical terms. Then I'd started visiting farmers, hoping to learn about the regenerative practices they were implementing to capture carbon and reduce emissions. But when it became clear to me that many of the communities with the strongest commitments to a regenerative food system were lacking secure access to land, I had to take a step back. It wasn't just individual farming practices standing in the way of agricultural climate solutions. It was our society's entire way of relating with land—and with each other. The extraction of carbon from soils was just one integral piece of a much larger process of extraction, a process that included the theft of indigenous lands, the forced enslavement of millions of Africans, and the extortion of immigrant labor. To repair the soil, we needed to repair it all.

Talking with Nguyen, Thapar, and Morningstar was a perfect opportunity to explore my original question about how much carbon could be drawn down through regenerative agriculture. Morningstar had recently been a full-time climate researcher, and Nguyen's professional background included generating climate models and analyzing soil carbon. Both had considerable experience practicing regenerative farming techniques, as did Thapar. But the longer we talked, the more we kept coming back to the intricate mechanics of an even deeper process: colonialism.

I had been preoccupied with a narrow question: how many tons of carbon can farmers suck out of the atmosphere and store underground? Pinning down this number proved elusive, as scientists pointed out the dizzying array of variables involved, from soil types to crop varieties to the length of time you assumed a particular form of management would be sustained. Truthfully, they admitted, we're just beginning to understand how to measure the movement of this tiny, consequential element. What we do know, however, is that carbon cycling works pretty well in healthy, functioning ecosystems.

Wondering if I'd failed to look at the most fundamental question underlying my whole project, I eventually asked Stephanie Morningstar a very unformed question. I'm sure the words didn't come out in this order, but the essence of it was this: so what *is* the climate crisis, I mean, really?

"This is ancestor work," Morningstar answered. "Everything that we're doing is ancestor work. Not just me, not just Black folks, not just people of color. Everybody."

Climate change signals a profound imbalance, Morningstar explained, rooted in the violent restructuring of relationships between people and land that lies at the very heart of this continent's history. This rupture disrupted the connections that make healthy, functioning ecosystems possible, including the connections that weave humans into the fabric of a place. That means the vital work of rebuilding soil carbon is inextricably woven together with the vital work of racial justice.

"What we are doing is we are healing our ancestral lineages," Morningstar clarified. "It's about going back to the root issues: Indigenous land dispossession and enslavement. How do we right those relationships between our own communities so that we can heal those things in this healing ground."

So healing the climate means healing land, I asked, trying to follow Morningstar's train of thought, and healing land means healing colonization?

"That's it," Morningstar said. "That's the work."

# Acknowledgments

It has been a deep honor and privilege to learn from the people who shared their insights and experiences with me as I researched this book. Latrice Tatsey, Terry Tatsey, Olivia Watkins, Aidee Guzman, Keu Moua, Nikiko Masumoto, Mai Nguyen, Neil Thapar, and Stephanie Morningstar have been extraordinarily generous and generative collaborators. Their collective wisdom is the heart, soul, and intellectual core of this book.

My writing was also informed by a number of other farmers, scholars, and advocates who patiently and thoughtfully answered my questions in interviews. I am grateful to all of these brilliant thought leaders for making time for these conversations and greatly enhancing my understanding of agriculture, regeneration, and justice: Asmeret Asefew Berhe, Tim Bowles, John Briggs, Tim Crews, Ruth Dahlquist-Willard, Sam Fuhlendorf, Mariah Gladstone, Steve Gliessman, Julie Grossman, Elizabeth Hoover, Nina Ichikawa, Kyran Kunkel, Heidi Liere, Jill Falcon Mackin, Bruce Maxwell, Erin Meier, Laura-Anne Minkoff-Zern, June Moua, Joji Muramoto, Gary Paul Nabhan, Leah Penniman, Stacy

Philpott, Paul Roge, Kristin Ruppell, Ricardo Salvador, Hila Shamon, Annie Shattuck, Paige Stanley, Aubrey Streit Krug, Kyle Tsukahira, Gabriel Valle, Sam Vang, and Wenjing Xu.

I am particularly thankful to Ricardo Salvador, and honored that such a powerful leader in the movement for ecological agriculture and social justice has graced this book with his thoughtful foreword.

Details matter. I'm forever grateful to dozens of colleagues who helped me track down written sources, connect with farmers and organizations, and figure out how to responsibly adapt my research during the coronavirus pandemic. Paula Yang and Keng Vang were instrumental in connecting me with Hmong farmers in the Central Valley and also provided critical translation and research assistance.

Lex Barlowe facilitated a key conversation among the primary collaborators in this book, helping us work through a collective decision about how to spend the proceeds. Lex held just the space we needed in order to, as Stephanie Morningstar put it, "amend the collective soil" out of which all of our work grows. (The initial proceeds from this book are helping to fund a BIPOC land access convergence, as well as a summer internship in regenerative grazing through the Piikani Lodge Health Institute).

In that spirit, we dedicate this book to everyone doing this work of healing and liberation on land, including those who've been at it for generations and those who are just beginning the journey.

I would not be a published author if not for the steady guidance of my mentor and literary agent, Jessica Papin. Over the course of nine years and three books, Jessica has taught me innumerable and invaluable lessons about how to navigate the publishing world and bring a writing project to fruition—and in a manner that is consistent with my values.

Among the things I am most grateful to Jessica for introducing me to Emily Turner, senior editor at Island Press. It was Emily who first encouraged me to write about land justice and community land trusts, and I could not ask for a better thought partner in developing this book.

What errors remain among these pages are due to my own limited understanding. For the errors that have been corrected along the way, I am profoundly thankful to Emily and copyeditor Elizabeth Farry—as well as freelance editor John Knight, ecosystem scientist Paige Stanley (who fixed a host of scientific mistakes in the draft), and two exceedingly kind colleagues, Tim Crews and Patrick Archie, who read over the original draft and provided feedback. Many errors were also corrected by the people quoted and featured in this book, who graciously read this material in draft and helped me represent their work more accurately and appropriately.

As we moved toward publication, I was fortunate to work with the team of thoroughgoing pros at Island Press, who crafted all the finishing touches of this book with care and ensured that it reached readers like you: David Miller, Sharis Simonian, Elise Ricotta, Julie Marshall, Jaime Jennings, Jason Leppig, Kyler Geoffroy, Rachel Miller, and Jen Hawse.

I am also deeply indebted to artist Patricia Wakida, whose prints appear on the cover and the title page of each chapter and have brought the words of this book to life.

It is an extraordinary privilege to have the time and space to commit to such a complex and rewarding project, and I am immensely grateful to my colleagues in the Environmental Studies Program at UC Santa Barbara for encouraging me and bolstering me with intellectual and moral support. I want to especially recognize the work of my financial colleagues past and present—Alex Radde, Boris Palencia, Vivian Stopple, Valerie Gonzalez, and Katie Feuerstine—who navigated complex layers of institutional process to ensure that my collaborators in this project were compensated. I also want to particularly thank my faculty mentor, David Pellow, for modeling the methodological integrity I aspire to, in which the principles of environmental justice are not just discussed in writing but practiced throughout the research process.

Beyond UC Santa Barbara, I am also supported by a worldwide network of agroecologists, writers, and geographers who are the most brilliant, selfless people you'll ever meet. I am particularly grateful to my frequent writing buddy and thought partner, Maywa Montenegro, who is not only a stalwart friend but is also responsible for seeding most of my better ideas.

The Carlisle, Holder, and Archie families have held me in the most loving embrace throughout my long, winding search for a deeper understanding of this world and my place within it.

I wrote this book during the coronavirus pandemic, physically distanced from all my friends and family members—except for one. It was Patrick Archie who singlehandedly transformed my quarantine into a writing retreat, insisting that we dedicate the brightest and most spacious room in our house for my work. For months, Patrick harvested and cooked many of my suppers—and much of the early development of this book happened in those long dinner conversations, as I drew heavily on Patrick's deep well of experience as a farmer and agroecologist. He has quite literally supported me every step of the way, and I could not ask for a better partner.

# Notes

## Introduction. Can Soil Really Save Us?

1 **"special report crafted by the Intergovernmental Panel on Climate Change"** Robin McKie, "We Must Change Food Production to Save the World, Says Leaked Report," *Guardian*, August 4, 2019, https://www.theguardian.com/environment/2019/aug/03/ipcc -land-use-food-prodution-key-to-climate-crisis-leaked-report.

2 **"a geoengineering technology that involved burning plants or biowaste"** David Roberts, "Sucking Carbon out of the Air Won't Solve Climate Change," *Vox*, July 16, 2018, https://www.vox.com /energy-and-environment/2018/6/14/17445622/direct-air-capture -air-to-fuels-carbondioxide -engineering.

2 **"proposed storing atmospheric CO$_2$ in carbon-rich minerals"** National Academies of Sciences, Engineering, and Medicine, "Carbon Mineralization of CO$_2$," in *Negative Emissions Technologies and Reliable Sequestration: A Research Agenda* (Washington, DC: National Academies Press, 2019), 247–318.

2 **"the media took to calling these direct air capture plants 'artificial trees.'"** Brian D'Souza, "Artificial Trees Could Help Save the Planet: Here's What You Need To Know About Them," *The Rising*, October 14, 2019, https://therising.co/2019/10/14/artificial-trees-could-help -save-the-planet-heres -what-you-need-to-know-about-them/.

2 **"soils constitute a carbon repository some three times as large"** Jorn Scharlemann, Edmund Tanner, Roland Hiederer, and Valerie Kapos, "Global Soil Carbon: Understanding and Managing the Largest Terrestrial Carbon Pool," *Carbon Management* 5, no. 1 (2014): 81–91.

3 **"three times larger than the amount of carbon currently in the atmosphere"** Todd A. Ontl and Lisa A. Schulte, "Soil Carbon Storage," *Nature Education Knowledge* 3, no. 10 (2012): 35.

3 **"some 133 gigatons of carbon have been released as a result"** Jonathan Sanderman, Tomislav Hengl, and Gregory J. Fiske, "Soil Carbon Debt of 12,000 Years of Human Land Use," *PNAS* 114, no. 36 (2017): 9575–80.

3 **"8 percent of total global soil carbon stocks"** Daisy Dunne, "World's Soils Have Lost 133bn Tonnes of Carbon Since the Dawn of Agriculture," Carbon Brief, August 25, 2017, https://www.carbon brief.org/worlds-soils-have-lost-133bn-tonnes-of-carbon-since-the -dawn-of-agriculture.

4 **"could offset 20 to 35 percent of greenhouse gas emissions"** Budiman Minasny, Brendan P. Malone, Alex B. McBratney, Denis A. Angers, Dominique Arrouays, Adam Chambers, Vincent Chaplot et al., "Soil Carbon 4 per Mille," *Geoderma* 492 (April 2017): 59–86.

4 **"large-scale investments from General Mills"** Gosia Wozniacka, "Can Regenerative Agriculture Reverse Climate Change? Big Food Is Banking on It," NBC News, October 29, 2019, https://www.nbc news.com/news/us-news/can-regenerative-agriculture-reverse -climate-change-big-food-banking -it-n1072941.

4 **"pegged regenerative agriculture's carbon offset potential at no more than 5 percent"** William H. Schlesinger and Ronald Amundson, "Managing for Soil Carbon Sequestration: Let's Get Realistic," *Global Change Biology* 25, no. 2 (2019): 386–89.

6 **"increase carbon levels near the soil surface but simultaneously decrease them at greater depth"** Timothy E. Crews and Brian E. Rumsey, "What Agriculture Can Learn from Native Ecosystems in Building Soil Organic Matter: A Review," *Sustainability* 9, no. 4 (2017): 578.

6 **"moving organic matter from one place to another"** Crews and Rumsey, "What Agriculture Can Learn from Native Ecosystems."

6 **"carbon from plant roots is five times more likely"** Robert B. Jackson, Kate Lajtha, Susan E. Crow, Gustaf Hugelius, Marc G. Kramer, and Gervasio Piñeiro, "The Ecology of Soil Carbon: Pools, Vulnerabilities, and Biotic and Abiotic Controls," *Annual Review of Ecology, Evolution, and Systematics* 48 (2017): 419–45.

13 **"incarcerated for years simply for the crime of their Japanese descent"** T. A. Frail, "The Injustice of Japanese-American Internment Camps Resonates Strongly to This Day," *Smithsonian*, January/February 2017, https://www.smithsonianmag.com/history/injustice-japanese -americans-internment-camps-resonates-strongly-180961422/.

## Chapter 1. Return of the Buffalo

19 **"80 percent of Montana's large vertebrates"** Loren Bird Rattler, "An Holistic Approach to Conservation, Agriculture Resource Management, and Food Sovereignty in Blackfeet Country." (lecture, 4th Annual Conference on Native Nutrition, Prior Lake, MN, September 16, 2019).

19 **"some thirty million buffalo"** Hannah Nordhaus, "Two Visions Collide amid Push to Restore Montana Plains," *National Geographic*, January 16, 2020, https://www.nationalgeographic.com/magazine /2020/02/two-visions-collide-amid-push-to-restore-montana-plain -feature/.

20 **"The historic range of the continent's largest mammal"** Nordhaus, "Two Visions Collide."

20 **"researchers have identified several species of frogs and other amphibians"** Interview with John Briggs, July 3, 2020.

20 **"a phenomenon ecologists refer to as compensatory growth"** Robin Wall Kimmerer, *Braiding Sweetgrass: Indigenous Wisdom, Scientific Knowledge and the Teachings of Plants* (Minneapolis, MN: Milkweed Editions, 2013), 163.

20 **"Buffalo grazing also delayed some grasses from setting seed"** W. R. Teague, S. L. Dowhower, S. A. Baker, N. Haile, P. B. DeLaune, and D. M. Conover, "Grazing Management Impacts on Vegetation, Soil Biota and Soil Chemical, Physical and Hydrological Properties in Tall Grass Prairie." *Agriculture, Ecosystems & Environment* 141, no. 3–4 (2011): 312, https://globalrangelands.org/topics/rangeland-ecology/ grass-growth.

20 **"an enzyme in buffalo saliva helped stimulate plant growth"** Kimmerer, *Braiding Sweetgrass*, 163.

20 **"grazing down the most dominant grasses to make space"** Interview with Samuel Fuhlendorf, June 17, 2020

21 **"The people knew what time of year the buffalo would move"** Interview with Terry Tatsey, July 28, 2020.

22 **"they even learned how to bring on these tender shoots"** Interview with Jill Falcon Mackin, July 28, 2020

22 **"sustained an impressive level of soil fertility"** Jane Mt. Pleasant and Robert F. Burt, "Estimating Productivity of Traditional Iroquoian Cropping Systems from Field Experiments and Historical Literature," *Journal of Ethnobiology* 30, no. 1 (2010): 53.

22 **"The quantity of corn which we found in store in this place . . ."** Jane Mt. Pleasant, "The Paradox of Plows and Productivity: An Agronomic Comparison of Cereal Grain Production under Iroquois Hoe Culture and European Plow Culture in the Seventeenth and Eighteenth Centuries," *Agricultural History* 85, no. 4 (2011): 471.

23 **"Haudenosaunee corn growers produced three to five times as much grain per acre"** Jane Mt. Pleasant, "A New Paradigm for Pre-Columbian Agriculture in North America," *Early American Studies* 13, no. 2 (2015): 401.

23 **"made up about a third of the plant species in their diet"** Gary Paul Nabhan, Erin C. Riordan, Laura Monti, Amadeo M. Rea, Benjamin T. Wilder, Exequiel Ezcurra, Jonathan B. Mabry, et al., "An Aridamerican Model for Agriculture in a Hotter, Water-Scarce World," *Plants, People, Planet* 2, no. 6 (2020): 1–13, https://doi.org/10.1002/ppp3.10129.

23 **"Indigenous Hawaiians carefully conserved the upland forest"** Kevin K. J. Chang, Charles K. H. Young, Brenda F Asuncion, Wallace K. Ito, Kawika B. Winter, and Wayne C. Tanaka, "Kua'Aina Ulu 'Auamo: Grassroots Growing through Shared Responsibility," in *Indigenous Food Sovereignty in the United States*, ed. Devon A. Mihesuah and Elizabeth Hoover (Norman: University of Oklahoma Press, 2019), 135.

23 **"the Hawaiian archipelago was largely self-sufficient in food"** Chang et al., "Kua'Aina Ulu 'Auamo," 126.

24 **"White men posed proudly atop piles of buffalo skulls"** See 1892 photo from the Detroit Public Library (Burton Historical Collection). The location was the grounds of the Michigan Carbon Works, Rougeville, Michigan.

25 **"the productivity of the Great Plains decreased some 71 percent"** Leah Penniman, *Farming While Black: Soul Fire Farm's Practical Guide to Liberation on the Land* (White River Junction, VT: Chelsea Green Publishing, 2018), 88; Evan A. Thaler, Isaac J. Larsen, and Qian Yu, "The Extent of Soil Loss across the US Corn Belt," *PNAS* 118, no. 8 (2021), https://www.pnas.org /content/118/8/e1922375118.

26 **"causing three hundred times as much warming"** Sabrina Shankman, "What Is Nitrous Oxide and Why Is It a Climate Threat?" *Inside Climate News*, September 11, 2019, https://insideclimatenews.org /news/11092019/nitrous-oxide-climate-pollutant-explainer-green house-gas-agriculture-livestock.

26 **"enough to circle the world ten times"** Tim Harford, "Why Barbed Wire—Yes, Barbed Wire—Was as Transformative as the Telephone," Ideas.Ted.Com, September 1, 2017, https://ideas.ted.com/why-barbed-wire-yes-barbed-wire-was-as-transformative-as-the-telephone/.

27 **"the scientific basis of these claims has since been questioned"** Nathan F. Sayre, "The Coyote-Proof Pasture Experiment: How Fences Replaced Predators and Labor on US Rangelands," *Progress in Physical Geography* 39, no. 5 (2015).

27 **"thousands of miles of fences were built"** Sayre, "Coyote-Proof Pasture Experiment," 589.

27 **"the Dawes Act"** Indian Land Tenure Foundation, "Land Tenure History," https://iltf.org/land-issues/history/.

27 **"kill the Indian, save the man"** Nick Estes, "The US Stole Generations of Indigenous Children to Open the West," *High Country News*, October 14, 2019, https://www.hcn.org/issues/51.17/indig enous-affairs-the-us-stole-generations-of-indigenous-children-to -open-the-west.

27 **"a violent system of discipline"** Estes, "The US Stole Generations of Indigenous Children."

28 **"what Chief Justice John Marshall termed 'domestic dependent' nations"** Cherokee Nation v. Georgia, 30 U.S. 1 (1831).

30 **"the tribal government began its first attempt to restore buffalo"** Rob Chaney, "Buffalo Rising: Iconic Anima's Return Feeds Renaissance of Blackfeet Culture," *Missoulian*, June 16, 2019, https://missoulian.com/news/local/buffalo-rising-iconic-animals -return-feeds-renaissance-of-blackfeet-culture/article_cb9ae40d -0874-52fc-8977-f583895f9e13.html.

33 **"to the Medicine Line Northern Tribes Buffalo Treaty"** Chris Smith, "The Future of Bison in Montana?" *Outdoor News Bulletin* 72, no. 6 (June 2018), https://wildlifemanagement.institute/ outdoor-news-bulletin/june-2018/future-bison-montana.

34 **"spurring a PBS documentary"** *Bring Them Home*, filmmaker Daniel Glick, 2016, https://watch.montanapbs.org/video/bring-them -homeiniskim-sjo1yk/.

34 **"some five hundred thousand of which were being raised for meat production"** Nordhaus, "Two Visions Collide."

34 **"just thirty thousand buffalo were in conservation herds"** Nordhaus, "Two Visions Collide."

34 **"only half of those in tribal hands"** Latrice Tatsey, "In-nii (Bison Bison): Are They Restoring Soil Health While Returning to Their Homelands?" (Land Resources and Environmental Science seminar series, Montana State University, April 23, 2018), http://landre-sources.montana.edu/archives/semi nar/spring2018.html.

35 **"In 2016, eighty-eight of them came back home"** Chaney, "Buffalo Rising."

36 **"There will be transformation of landscape in Glacier National Park..."** Joe Huisinga, "Blackfeet Nation Works to Restore Bison on the Rocky Mountain Front," MTN News, November 3, 2018, https:// www.krtv.com/news/montana-and-regional-news/2018/11/03/black feet-nation-works-to-restore-bison-on-the-rocky-mountain-front/.

37 **"creating its own Agricultural Resource Management Plan"** Bird Rattler, "An Holistic Approach."

37 **"funded by a $2 million grant"** Foundation for Food and Agriculture Research, "FFAR Awards 100th Grant to Support Sustainable Agriculture in Black feet Nation," July 10, 2019, https://foundationfar .org/news/ffar-awards-100th-grant-to-support-sustainable-agricul ture-in-blackfeet-nation/.

42  **"One of the hypotheses Tatsey is keen to explore"** Some of the research Tatsey is building on: Stephen A. Goff and Harry J. Klee, "Plant Volatile Compounds: Sensory Cues for Health and Nutritional Value?" *Science* 311, no. 5762 (February 2006).

43  **"The project is controversial"** Nate Hegyi, "The Next Yellowstone: How Big Money Is Building a New Kind of National Park," Yellowstone Public Radio, December 20, 2019, https://www.ypradio.org/post/next-yellowstone-how-big-money-building-new-kind-national-park#stream/0.

48  **"released over fifty billion tons of greenhouse gases"** Timothy E. Crews and Brian E. Rumsey, "What Agriculture Can Learn from Native Ecosystems in Building Soil Organic Matter: A Review," *Sustainability* 9, no. 4 (2017): 582.

48  **"all reciprocal relations [are] reduced to a 'keep out' sign."** Kimmerer, *Braiding Sweetgrass*, 327.

49  **"The aromatic perennial responds to traditional harvesting"** Kimmerer, *Braiding Sweetgrass*, 163.

49  **"the Hidatsa and Mandan only farmed low-lying areas"** Gilbert L. Wilson, *Buffalo Bird Woman's Garden: Agriculture of the Hidatsa Indians* (1917; repr., St. Paul: Minnesota Historical Society Press, 1987), https://digital.library.upenn.edu/women/buffalo/garden/garden.html.

49  **"They minimized disturbance by making semipermanent mounds"** Mt. Pleasant, "A New Paradigm," 411.

49  **"Reciprocity is a matter of keeping the gift in motion . . ."** Kimmerer, *Braiding Sweetgrass*, 184.

51  **"releasing several gigatons of carbon into the atmosphere every year"** "Forest Protection," Project Drawdown, https://drawdown.org/solutions/forest-protection, excerpted from Paul Hawken, ed., *Drawdown: The Most Comprehensive Plan Ever Proposed to Reverse Global Warming* (New York: Penguin, 2017).

51  **"has failed to achieve even modest carbon storage"** Robert Heilmayr, Cristian Echeverría, and Eric F. Lambin, "Impacts of Chilean Forest Subsidies on Forest Cover, Carbon and Biodiversity," *Nature Sustainability* 3 (2020): 701–09.

## Chapter 2. Black Land Matters

53 **"Black Land Matters"** A phrase I am borrowing from Leah Penniman, who uses it as the title of the introduction to her book, *Farming While Black*.

54 **"the twenty-fourth annual Negro Farmers Conference"** Allen Jones, "Improving Rural Life for Blacks: The Tuskegee Negro Farmers' Conference, 1892–1915," *Agricultural History* 65, no. 2 (1991): 113.

55 **"Hundreds of similar gatherings were held across the South"** Jones, "Improving Rural Life for Blacks," 112.

55 **"925,000 Black farmers owned the land they cultivated"** Leah Penniman, *Farming While Black: Soul Fire Farm's Practical Guide to Liberation on the Land* (White River Junction, VT: Chelsea Green Publishing, 2018), 269.

55 **"Black families gained title to some four hundred thousand acres of land"** Dánia C. Davy, Savonala Horne, Tracy Lloyd McCurty, and Edward "Jerry" Pennick, "Resistance," in *Land Justice: Re-imagining Land, Food, and the Commons*, ed. Justine M. Williams and Eric Holt-Giménez (Oakland: Food First Books, 2017), 40–60.

55 **"most of the land was seized from Black families"** Penniman, *Farming While Black*, 267.

55 **"laws prohibiting Black people from owning or even leasing property"** Laura-Anne Minkoff-Zern, *The New American Farmer: Immigration, Race, and the Struggle for Sustainability* (Cambridge, MA: MIT Press, 2019), 34.

56 **"arrested at harvest season and forced into contract labor as punishment"** Penniman, *Farming While Black*, 266–67.

56 **"allowed landowners to retain their labor force indefinitely"** Mark Hersey, *My Work Is That of Conservation: An Environmental Biography of George Washington Carver* (Athens: University of Georgia Press, 2011), 72.

56 **"More than 4,000 African Americans were lynched between 1877 and 1950"** Penniman, *Farming While Black*, 267.

56 **"corroborating the dispossession of 406 Black landowners and a total of 24,000 acres"** Todd Lewan and Dolores Barclay, "Torn from the Land: Black Americans' Farmland Taken through

Cheating, Intimidation, Even Murder," part 1, Associated Press, December 2, 2001, https://archive.seattletimes.com/archive/?date=20011202&slug=torn02.

56 **"Over half the cases involved violence"** Todd Lewan and Dolores Barclay, "Torn from the Land: Landownership Made Blacks Targets of Violence and Murder," part 2, Associated Press, December 3, 2001, https://theau thenticvoice.org/mainstories/tornfromtheland / torn_part2/.

56 **"thousands of additional reports of land-takings . . ."** Lewan and Barclay, "Torn From the Land," part 1.

57 **"By 1890, Black people had purchased 120,738 farms."** Penniman, *Farming While Black*, 258.

57 **"By 1900, a quarter of Black farmers owned the land they farmed."** Minkoff-Zern, *New American Farmer*, 35.

57 **"Black land ownership had nearly reached sixteen million acres"** Vann R. Newkirk II, "The Great Land Robbery," *Atlantic*, September 2019, https://www.theatlantic.com/magazine/archive/2019/09/this-land-was-our-land/594742/.

57 **"98 percent of Black landowners would be dispossessed"** Newkirk, "The Great Land Robbery."

57 **"accelerate the displacement and impoverishment of the Negro farmer."** Newkirk, "The Great Land Robbery."

58 **"many Black farmers were flatly denied the government loans"** Penniman, *Farming While Black*, 268.

58 **"they were smaller than those offered to White applicants"** Newkirk, "The Great Land Robbery."

58 **"private lenders followed similar patterns of discrimination"** Newkirk, "The Great Land Robbery."

58 **"an area the size of New York's Central Park erased with each sunset"** Newkirk, "The Great Land Robbery."

59 **"Such partition sales have accounted for over half of Black land loss"** Penniman, *Farming While Black*, 268.

59 **"nearly all these lands are now owned by White individuals or corporations"** Newkirk, "The Great Land Robbery."

59  **"$500 million, the largest civil rights settlement in history"** Penniman, *Farming While Black*, 284.

59  **"would eventually reach a total of $2 billion"** Newkirk, "The Great Land Robbery."

59  **"a small fraction of lost property value and income"** Newkirk, "The Great Land Robbery."

59  **"When they steal your land . . ."** Lewan and Barclay, "Torn from the Land," part 1.

63  **"North Carolina has become the epicenter of the wood pellet industry"** Saul Elbein, "Slow Burn: Europe Uses Tons of NC Trees as Fuel. Will This Solve Climate Change?" *News and Observer* (Raleigh, NC), January 3, 2020, https://www.newsobserver.com/news/business/article238395173.html.

64  **"much of North Carolina's biodiversity is being lost"** Reid Creager, "North Carolina's Fading Forests," *Charlotte Observer*, March 27, 2016, https://www.charlotteobserver.com/news/science-technology/article67735547.html.

64  **"Scientists predict another 5.5 million acres of trees will fall"** North Carolina State University Cooperative Extension, "Forest Lost to Urban Development," Going Native: Urban Landscaping for Wildlife with Native Plants, https://projects.ncsu.edu/goingnative/whygo/habloss.html.

64  **"global biodiversity losses equaling a mass extinction."** Xingli Giam, "Global Biodiversity Loss from Tropical Deforestation," *PNAS* 114, no. 23. (June 6, 2017): 5777.

64  **"some 10 to 15 percent of global carbon emissions"** "Forest Protection," Project Drawdown, https://drawdown.org/solutions/forest-protection, excerpted from Paul Hawken, ed., *Drawdown: The Most Comprehensive Plan Ever Proposed to Reverse Global Warming* (New York: Penguin, 2017).

64  **"In addition to protecting watersheds and soils, trees provide significant wildlife habitat"** Michele M. Schoeneberger, Gary Bentrup, and Toral Patel-Weynand, eds., *Agroforestry: Enhancing Resiliency in U.S. Agricultural Landscapes Under Changing Conditions*, US Forest Service Gen. Tech. Report WO-96. (Washington, DC: United States Department of Agriculture, November 2017), https://www.fs.fed.us/research/publications/gtr/gtr_wo96.pdf.

66  **"share stress signals to alert each other to deforestation"** Valentina Lagomarsino, "Exploring the Underground Network of Trees—The Nervous System of the Forest," *Science in the News*, Harvard University Graduate School of Arts and Sciences, May 6, 2019, http://sitn .hms.harvard.edu/flash/2019/exploring-the-underground-network -of-trees-the-nervous-system-of-the-forest/.

67  **"most African lands were managed in common"** Kwasi Densu, "Theoretical and Historical Perspectives on Agroecology and African American Farmers," in *Land and Power: Sustainable Agriculture and African Americans*, ed. Jeffrey L. Jordan, Edward Pennick, Walter A. Hill, and Robert Zabawa (College Park, MD: SARE Outreach, 2009), 100.

67  **"the same word used for family and community"** Densu, "Theoretical and Historical Perspectives," 99.

67  **"This historical legacy of cooperation proved essential to surviving"** Penniman, *Farming While Black*, 265; Monica M. White, *Freedom Farmers: Agricultural Resistance and the Black Freedom Movement* (Chapel Hill, University of North Carolina Press, 2018), xvii.

67  **"Mutual aid was important to everyday subsistence"** Judith A. Carney, "Subsistence in the Plantationocene: Dooryard Gardens, Agrobiodiversity, and the Subaltern Economies of Slavery," *Journal of Peasant Studies* (2020): 10.

68  **"reestablishing the African village in the United States"** Davy et al., "Resistance," 155.

68  **"the Colored Farmers' Alliance"** White, *Freedom Farmers*, 14.

68  **"the first scholar to research Black cooperatives in the United States"** White, *Freedom Farmers*, 51.

68  **"a continuous and hidden history . . ."** White, *Freedom Farmers*, 51.

68  **"DuBois documented an underground informal economy"** White, *Freedom Farmers*, 53.

68  **"founding the Negro Cooperative Guild in 1918"** White, *Freedom Farmers*, 58.

68  **"Tomorrow we may work for ourselves . . ."** White, *Freedom Farmers*, 56.

69  **"Hamer was born in 1917"** Details of Hamer's early life are drawn from White, *Freedom Farmers*, 66.

69 **"Hamer began registering Black voters in 1962"** White, *Freedom Farmers*, 66–67.

69 **"Hamer became a central figure in the civil rights movement"** White, *Freedom Farmers*, 67.

69 **"she sought to create a cooperative institution"** White, *Freedom Farmers*, 71.

70 **"Hamer's Freedom Farm Cooperative grew into a 692-acre farm"** White, *Freedom Farmers*, 73.

70 **"included a community garden for subsistence, as well as revenue-raising enterprises"** White, *Freedom Farmers*, 76.

70 **"Perhaps Hamer's most significant innovation was the 'pig bank'"** White, *Freedom Farmers*, 77.

70 **"an eighty-unit affordable housing development"** White, *Freedom Farmers*, 78.

70 **"one of the nation's first Head Start programs"** White, *Freedom Farmers*, 79.

70 **"a sewing cooperative"** White, *Freedom Farmers*, 80.

70 **"a tool lending library"** White, *Freedom Farmers*, 82.

70 **"If you have a pig in your backyard . . ."** White, *Freedom Farmers*, 65.

70 **"The Federation of Southern Cooperatives—'the co-op of co-ops'—was born."** White, *Freedom Farmers*, 99.

70 **"the federation chipped away the financial power structure"** White, *Freedom Farmers*, 104.

71 **"The federation also collectively marketed Black farmers' crops"** White, *Freedom Farmers*, 107.

71 **"home to 134 member cooperatives from fourteen southern states"** White, *Freedom Farmers*, 101.

71 **"one-third of which were focused on agriculture"** White, *Freedom Farmers*, 102.

71 **"provided technical assistance to members and developed demonstration farms"** White, *Freedom Farmers*, 102–03.

71 **"constructed fourteen solar greenhouses and initiated a revolving loan fund"** White, *Freedom Farmers*, 106–07.

71 **"promoted and helped finance water conservation infrastructure"** White, *Freedom Farmers*, 106–07.

71 **"controlled one million acres of land"** White, *Freedom Farmers*, 108.

71 **"White elites took extraordinary measures to undermine the federation's power"** White, *Freedom Farmers*, 112–14.

71 **"Alabama state troopers stopped a fleet of refrigerated trucks"** White, *Freedom Farmers*, 114.

72 **"the Sherrods won the largest settlement in the *Pigford* lawsuit"** Penniman, *Farming While Black*, 13.

73 **"a prophet of sustainable agriculture"** Hersey, *My Work Is That of Conservation*, 2.

73 **"the most widely recognized and admired Black man in America"** Hersey, *My Work Is That of Conservation*, 1.

74 **"Carver was born into slavery in Missouri"** White, *Freedom Farmers*, 39.

74 **"His adoptive mother began requiring Carver to empty his pockets"** Hersey, *My Work Is That of Conservation*, 12.

74 **"a hidden wildflower garden in the woods"** White, *Freedom Farmers*,40.

74 **"Carver eventually made his way to Simpson College"** Hersey, *My Work Is That of Conservation*, 21.

74 **"recommended he pursue a degree at the Iowa Agricultural College"** Hersey, *My Work Is That of Conservation*, 22.

74 **"not only the first Black student to attend the Iowa Agricultural College"** Hersey, *My Work Is That of Conservation*, 28.

74 **"he was introduced to the emerging field of ecology"** Hersey, *My Work Is That of Conservation*, 37.

74 **"Carver stayed on at the college to pursue a graduate degree"** White, *Freedom Farmers*, 40.

75 **"A young cook at Ames recalled sharing in the bounty of mushrooms"** Peter Duncan Burchard, *George Washington Carver: For His Time and Ours* Special History Study: Natural History Related to George Washington Carver National Monument, Diamond, Missouri (2005), 44, https://www.nps.gov/gwca/learn/management/upload/GWC-For-His-Time-Ours-Spec-History-Study.pdf.

75 "coauthored a pair of articles in mycology journals" Hersey, *My Work Is That of Conservation*, 44.

75 "Carver also collaborated with one of Pammel's former students" Hersey, *My Work Is That of Conservation*, 44.

75 "Booker T. Washington wrote to offer Carver a position" Hersey, *My Work Is That of Conservation*, 45–46.

75 "believed it was his God-given duty" Hersey, *My Work Is That of Conservation*, 45–46.

75 "the only African American who held an advanced degree in agricultural science" Hersey, *My Work Is That of Conservation*, 1.

75 "placed in charge of the institute's new agricultural experiment station and its outreach" White, *Freedom Farmers*, 41–45.

75 "manage the university's 2,300 acres of farmland and teach up to six classes" Hersey, *My Work Is That of Conservation*, 86–87.

76 "intended to show the impoverished tenant farmers of Macon County" Hersey, *My Work Is That of Conservation*, 98.

76 "Carver was perhaps even more enamored of the cowpea" White, *Freedom Farmers*, 48; Hersey, *My Work Is That of Conservation*, 131.

76 "his first experiment, beginning in 1897" Hersey, *My Work Is That of Conservation*, 126.

76 "By 1905, he had managed to curb the erosion" Hersey, *My Work Is That of Conservation*, 126.

77 "increasingly eclipsed discussion of organic methods" Mark D. Hersey, "The Transformation of George Washington Carver's Environmental Vision, 1896–1918," in Jordan et al., *Land and Power*, 61.

77 "one of the first agricultural scientists to question US agriculture's turn toward chemicals" White, *Freedom Farmers*, 46.

77 "nearly 95 percent of Black farmers were tenants or sharecroppers" Hersey, *My Work Is That of Conservation*, 151.

77 "would cost $720 for a twenty-acre farm" Hersey, *My Work Is That of Conservation*, 135.

77 "Crop rotation and cover cropping were out" Hersey, *My Work Is That of Conservation*, 202.

77 "Most sharecroppers couldn't afford well-bred livestock" Hersey, *My Work Is That of Conservation*, 203.

78  **"Nature has provided us with an almost innumerable variety of wild vegetables . . ."** Hersey, *My Work Is That of Conservation*, 132.

78  **"sixty species collected by Carver"** Burchard, *George Washington Carver*, 50.

78  **"His very first bulletin at the Tuskegee experiment station"** Hersey, *My Work Is That of Conservation*, 127.

78  **"We are richer than we think we are . . ."** Hersey, *My Work Is That of Conservation*, 143.

78  **"the 'organic unity' of the ecosystem"** Hersey, "Transformation of George Washington Carver's Environmental Vision," 68.

79  **"mutual relationship of the animal, mineral, and vegetable kingdoms"** White, *Freedom Farmers*, 46.

79  **"natural fertilizer factory . . ."** Hersey, *My Work Is That of Conservation*, 139.

79  **"Carver put composting at the center of his research program"** White, *Freedom Farmers*, 47.

79  **"astonishing improvements in the water-holding capacity of his fields"** White, *Freedom Farmers*, 47.

79  **"Nature's choicest fertilizer"** John S. Ferrell, "George Washington Carver: A Blazer of Trails to a Sustainable Future," in Jordan et al., *Land and Power*, 18.

79  **"tried to get the entire Tuskegee campus to switch from commercial fertilizers to compost"** Hersey, *My Work Is That of Conservation*, 140–41.

79  **"We know that commercial fertilizers will stimulate . . ."** Hersey, *My Work Is That of Conservation*, 141.

80  **"Carver brought the request to Tuskegee's council"** Hersey, *My Work Is That of Conservation*, 141.

80  **"grew by a factor of three"** Hersey, *My Work Is That of Conservation*, 195.

80  **"promoted a parallel and hidden Black subsistence economy"** Hersey, *My Work Is That of Conservation*, 144.

80  **"a good plate of dandelion greens . . ."** Hersey, *My Work Is That of Conservation*, 132–33.

80 **"This line of education . . ."** George Washington Carver's acceptance letter to Booker T. Washington, Tuskegee job, quoted in White, *Freedom Farmers*, 41.

81 **"African Indigenous agriculture was as diverse as the continent itself"** Judith A. Carney and Richard N. Rosomoff, *In the Shadow of Slavery: Africa's Botanical Legacy in the Atlantic World* (Berkeley: University of California Press, 2009), 7.

81 **"Trees were central to African Indigenous farming"** Carney and Rosomoff, *In the Shadow of Slavery*, 23.

81 **"farmers protected a number of valued tree species"** Owusu Bandele and Gail Myers, "Roots!" in Williams and Holt-Giménez, *Land Justice*, 101–02.

81 **"Among these species"** Carney and Rosomoff, *In the Shadow of Slavery*, 23.

81 **"[transformed] a rainforest into a food forest."** Carney and Rosomoff, *In the Shadow of Slavery*, 25.

81 **"pruned tree crops to allow adequate light for crops planted below"** Bandele and Myers, "Roots!" 101–02.

82 **"have developed numerous polycultures of trees and row crops"** Penniman, *Farming While Black*, 123.

82 **"Africans brought staple foods with them"** Penniman, *Farming While Black*, 149; Carney, "Subsistence in the Plantationocene," 2.

82 **"Dooryard gardens"** Carney, "Subsistence in the Plantationocene," 6.

82 **"White observers marveled at the bounteous gardens"** Carney, "Subsistence in the Plantationocene," 6.

82 **"islands of agrobiodiversity disrupting a sea of commodity monoculture"** Carney, "Subsistence in the Plantationocene," 7.

82 **"the botanical gardens of the Atlantic world's dispossessed"** Carney and Rosomoff, *In the Shadow of Slavery*, 135.

82 **"forest gardens would help their stewards transform dispossession into resistance"** Kimberly N. Ruffin, "York, Harriet, and George: Writing African American Ecological Ancestors," in Jordan et al., *Land and Power*, 55.

83 **"Tubman's knowledge of wild plants and herbal medicine"** Penniman, *Farming While Black*, 190.

83　**"monocultural crops are being used in a 'predatory system'"** Tania Murray Li, "After the Land Grab: Infrastructural Violence and the 'Mafia System' in Indonesia's Oil Palm Plantation Zones," *Geoforum* 96, (November 2018): 329.

83　**"the plantations are back"** Li, "After the Land Grab," 328.

83　**"If policies to incentivize tree plantations are poorly designed or poorly enforced . . ."** Harrison Tasoff, "Forgetting the Forest for the Trees," *The Current*, June 25, 2020, https://www.news.ucsb.edu/2020/019951/forgetting-forest-trees.

84　**"the policy has failed to increase carbon storage"** Robert Heilmayr, Cristian Echeverría, and Eric F. Lambin, "Impacts of Chilean Forest Subsidies on Forest Cover, Carbon and Biodiversity," *Nature Sustainability* 3 (2020): 701–09.

85　**"They were also central to developing many of the policies"** Nadra Nittle, "Tracy McCurty Has Worked a Long Time to See Historic Wrongs Righted for Black Farmers," *Civil Eats*, March 29, 2021, https://civileats.com/2021/03/29/tracy-mccurty-has-worked-a-long-time-to-see-historic-wrongs-righted-for-black-farmers/.

88　**"what Vandermeer and Perfecto came to refer to as 'nature's matrix'"** Ivette Perfecto, John Vandermeer, and Angus Wright, *Nature's Matrix: Linking Agriculture, Biodiversity Conservation and Food Sovereignty*, 2nd ed. (New York: Routledge, 2019).

88　**"If Black women were free . . ."** Keeanga-Yamahtta Taylor, "Until Black Women Are Free, None of Us Will Be Free," *New Yorker*, July 20, 2020, https://www.newyorker.com/news/our-columnists/until-blackwomen-are-free-none-of-us-will-be-free.

## Chapter 3. Hidden Hotspots of Biodiversity

92　**"One-third of the produce grown in the United States"** Mark Bittman, "Everyone Eats There," *New York Times*, October 10, 2012, https://www.nytimes.com/2012/10/14/magazine/californias-central-valley-land-of-a-billion-vegetables.html.

94　**"two times as many types of arbuscular mycorrhizal fungi"** Aidee Guzman, Marisol Montes, Leslie Hutchins, Gisel DeLaCerda, Paula Yang, Anne Kakouridis, Ruth M. Dahlquist-Willard, Mary K. Firestone, Timothy Bowles, and Claire Kremen, "Crop Diversity Enriches

Arbuscular Mycorrhizal Fungal Communities in an Intensive Agricultural Landscape," *New Phytologist* 231, no. 1 (2021), https://nph.onlinelibrary.wiley.com/doi/full /10.1111/nph.17306.

96 **"outperforms the combined yields of the three crops when they are grown by themselves"** Stephen R. Gliessman, "Agroecology: Roots of Resistance" chap. 2 in *Agroecology: A Transdisciplinary, Participatory, and Action-Oriented Approach*, ed. V. Ernesto Méndez, Christopher M. Bacon, Roseann Cohen, and Stephen R. Gliessman (N.p.: Taylor & Francis, 2015), 29.

96 **"played a key role in the maintenance and regeneration of biological diversity"** Mariana Benítez, Juan Fornoni, Luis García-Barrios, and Rafael López, "Dynamical Networks in Agroecology: The Milpa as a Model System," in *Frontiers in Ecology, Evolution and Complexity*, ed. Mariana Benítez, Octavio Miramontes, and Alfonso Valiente-Banuet (Mexico City: CopIt -arXives, 2014), 14.

96 **"the foundation of food security . . ."** Benítez et al., "Dynamical Networks in Agroecology," 11.

97 **"dates back over ten thousand years ago"** Alba González-Jacome, "Analysis of Tropical Home Gardens through an Agroecology and Anthropological Ecology Perspective," in Méndez et al., *Agroecology*, 235.

97 **"Archaeologists have found their remains up and down Mexico"** González-Jacome, "Analysis of Tropical Home Gardens," 236.

97 **"composed of a mixture of wild plants and 'incidentally' domesticated species"** González-Jacome, "Analysis of Tropical Home Gardens," 236.

98 **"the closest expression is *MeyajbilK'aax* . . ."** Francisco J. Rosado-May, "The Intercultural Origin of Agroecology," chap. 8 in Méndez et al., *Agroecology*, 132.

98 **"some of the most complex agricultural landscapes in the world"** Stephen R. Gliessman, *Agroecology: The Ecology of Sustainable Food Systems*, 3rd ed. (Boca Raton, FL: CRC Press, 2015), 232.

98 **"At the ground level"** Devon G. Peña, *Mexican Americans and the Environment: Tierra y Vida* (Tucson: University of Arizona Press, 2005), 51.

98 **"Small livestock such as turkeys, chickens, and pigs"** Gliessman, "Agroecology: Roots of Resistance," 30.

98  **"replicate the structure and function of the surrounding rainforest"** Gliessman, "Agroecology: Roots of Resistance," 30.

98  **"They are extremely biodiverse"** Gliessman, "Agroecology: Roots of
Resistance," 31.

104  **"Born in 1913 in Tlaxcala"** Marta Astier, Jorge Quetzal Argueta,
Quetzalcóatl Orozco-Ramírez, María V. González, Jaime Morales,
Peter R. W. Gerritsen, Miguel A. Escalona, Francisco J. Rosado-May,
Julio Sánchez-Escudero, Tomas Martínez Saldaña, Cristobal Sánchez-
Sánchez, et al., "Back to the Roots: Understanding Current Agroecological Movement, Science, and Practice in Mexico," *Agroecology and
Sustainable Food Systems* 41, no. 3–4 (2017): 333.

104  **"the smallest and perhaps the poorest state in Central Mexico"**
Efraím Hernández Xolocotzi, "Experiences Leading to a Greater
Emphasis on Man in Ethnobotanical Studies," *Economic Botany* 41,
no. 1 (1987): 6.

104  **"earned a bachelor's degree in applied agriculture at Cornell University"** Xolocotzi, "Experiences Leading to a Greater Emphasis on
Man," 6.

104  **"accepted to a graduate program at Harvard University"** Astier
et al., "Back to the Roots," 333.

104  **"Xolocotzi abandoned his PhD program to return home to
Mexico"** Xolocotzi, "Experiences Leading to a Greater Emphasis
on Man," 6.

104  **"it was Xolocotzi's job to collect as many varieties as he could
find"** Interview with Steve Gliessman, April 6, 2020.

105  **"Mexican president Lázaro Cárdenas was implementing a massive
land reform"** Tore C. Olsson, *Agrarian Crossings: Reformers and the
Remaking of the US and Mexican Countryside* (Princeton, NJ: Princeton University Press, 2017), 122.

105  **"Cárdenas ultimately redistributed over twenty million hectares"**
Laura-Anne Minkoff-Zern, *The New American Farmer: Immigration,
Race, and the Struggle for Sustainability* (Cambridge, MA: MIT Press,
2019), 141–42.

105  **"the Rockefeller Foundation dreamed up the Mexican Agricultural Program"** Olsson, *Agrarian Crossings*, 122.

105 **"focused on 'inexpensive and feasible' methods"** Olsson, *Agrarian Crossings*, 144–45.

105 **"sought to produce seeds that could be saved and replanted by farmers"** Olsson, *Agrarian Crossings*, 144.

106 **"far less enthusiastic about the ejido system"** Olsson, *Agrarian Crossings*, 146.

106 **"Alemán preferred 'hybrid' seeds"** Olsson, *Agrarian Crossings*, 149.

106 **"global food security emerged as an urgent political issue"** Olsson, *Agrarian Crossings*, 152.

106 **"asked to provide a universally replicable model for how to feed the world"** Olsson, *Agrarian Crossings*, 153.

106 **"began advocating for dramatic funding increases"** Olsson, *Agrarian Crossings*, 152.

106 **"not economical"** Olsson, *Agrarian Crossings*, 151.

106 **"after working for agribusiness giants like DuPont"** Olsson, *Agrarian Crossings*, 151.

107 **"a new research center in the heart of the northern Mexican wheat belt"** Olsson, *Agrarian Crossings*, 153–54.

107 **"Mexican wheat farmers were mostly wealthy elites"** Olsson, *Agrarian Crossings*, 154.

107 **"Borlaug bred hybrid wheat seeds that produced incredible yields"** Olsson, *Agrarian Crossings*, 154.

107 **"exported to Colombia, India, Chile, and the Philippines"** Olsson, *Agrarian Crossings*, 155.

107 **"Borlaug would win the Nobel Peace Prize in 1970"** Olsson, *Agrarian Crossings*, 156.

107 **"he did indeed find the incredible diversity of corn genetics"** Xolocotzi, "Experiences Leading to a Greater Emphasis on Man," 7.

107 **"four of the ten most biodiverse countries in the world"** Rhett A. Butler, "The Top 10 Most Biodiverse Countries," *Mongabay*, May 21, 2016, https://news.mongabay.com/2016/05/top-10-bio diverse-countries/.

107 **"in the 'Center of Origin' where corn was first domesticated"** Peña, *Mexican Americans and the Environment*, 45–46.

107 **"Xolocotzi strayed from his stated mission to gather 'raw material'"** Xolocotzi, "Experiences Leading to a Greater Emphasis on Man."

108 **"The Green Revolution, Xolocotzi observed, was not useful to the majority"** Gliessman, "Agroecology: Roots of Resistance," 26–27; interview with Steve Gliessman, April 6, 2020.

108 **"appointed to a prestigious professorship at the National School of Agriculture"** Astier et al., "Back to the Roots," 333.

108 **"was supposed to teach plant taxonomy and economic botany"** Xolocotzi, "Experiences Leading to a Greater Emphasis on Man," 7–11.

108 **"the mutual relations between man and plants"** Xolocotzi, "Experiences Leading to a Greater Emphasis on Man," 11.

108 **"speaking proudly about his Indigenous Nahuatl heritage"** Rosado-May, "Intercultural Origin of Agroecology," 132.

108 **"the Green Revolution was deepening its grip on Mexican agriculture"** Gliessman, "Agroecology: Roots of Resistance," 26.

109 **"Maestro Xolo"** Irene H. Reti, "Stephen R. Gliessman: Alfred E. Heller Professor of Agroecology, UC Santa Cruz," UC Santa Cruz: Regional History Project, 2010, https://library.ucsc.edu/reg-hist/stephen-r-gliessman-alfred-e-heller-professor-of-agroecology-uc-santa-cruz.

109 **"Xolocotzi held a national seminar on the 'Agroecosystems of Mexico'"** Gliessman, "Agroecology: Roots of Resistance," 24–26.

109 **"the bank hoped to turn the region into "'the new granary of Mexico'"** Gliessman, "Agroecology: Roots of Resistance," 28; "little cement block houses" is from Gliessman interview.

110 **"understood that instead of continuing to focus so much attention on getting rid of diseases . . ."** Gliessman, *Agroecology: The Ecology of Sustainable Food Systems.*

110 **"concerned about the Inter-American Development Bank's plans"** Gliessman, *Agroecology: The Ecology of Sustainable Food Systems.*

111 **"the traditional Mayan agriculture that was all around"** Gliessman, "Agroecology: Roots of Resistance," 28.

111 **"When these ecologists teamed up with Xolocotzi and his research group"** Gliessman, "Agroecology: Roots of Resistance," 28.

112 **"They conducted thorough studies of milpas"** Gliessman, "Agroecology: Roots of Resistance," 29.

112 **"counted species and measured leaf cover in tropical home gardens"** Gliessman, "Agroecology: Roots of Resistance," 31.

112 **"also turned their attention to the wetland agriculture"** Gliessman, *Agroecology: The Ecology of Sustainable Food Systems*, 71.

112 **"an elegant community engineering project to cultivate the swampy soils"** Gliessman, *Agroecology: The Ecology of Sustainable Food Systems*, 71.

112 **"farmers had excavated massive trenches of soil"** Timothy E. Crews and Stephen R. Gliessman, "Raised Field Agriculture in Tlaxcala, Mexico: An Ecosystem Perspective on Maintenance of Soil Fertility," *American Journal of Alternative Agriculture* 6, no. 1 (1991): 9.

112 **"planted with the same sort of diverse polycultures"** Gliessman, *Agroecology: The Ecology of Sustainable Food Systems*, 71–72.

113 **"farmers planted a variety of trees, particularly alders"** Crews and Gliessman, "Raised Field Agriculture in Tlaxcala, Mexico," 14.

113 **"moisture could simply travel up to the plant roots through 'capillarity'"** Gliessman, *Agroecology: The Ecology of Sustainable Food Systems*, 72.

113 **"combined the functions of an irrigation ditch and a compost pile"** Crews and Gliessman, "Raised Field Agriculture in Tlaxcala, Mexico," 15.

113 **"added to this reservoir of organic matter"** Gliessman, *Agroecology: The Ecology of Sustainable Food Systems*, 72.

113 **"the community gathered to dredge the canals"** Crews and Gliessman, "Raised Field Agriculture in Tlaxcala, Mexico," 15.

113 **"largely self-reliant in energy and nutrients"** Crews and Gliessman, "Raised Field Agriculture in Tlaxcala, Mexico," 9.

113 **"'floating gardens,' or *chinampas*"** Ivette Perfecto, John Vandermeer, and Angus Wright, *Nature's Matrix: Linking Agriculture, Biodiversity Conservation and Food Sovereignty*, 2nd ed. (New York: Routledge, 2019), 111.

113 **"Aquatic plants—particularly water hyacinth—provided continuous organic matter"** Roland Ebel, "Chinampas: An Urban Farming Model of the Aztecs and a Potential Solution for Modern Megalopolis," *HortTechnology* 30, no. 1 (2019): 16.

113 **"Originally developed by the Mayans"** Peña, *Mexican Americans and the Environment*, 45.

114 **"vast network of raised field systems"** D. Renard, J. Iriarte, J. J. Birk, S. Rostain, B. Glaser, and D. McKey, "Ecological Engineers Ahead of Their Time: The Functioning of Pre-Columbian Raised-Field Agriculture and Its Potential Contributions to Sustainability Today," *Ecological Engineering* 45 (2012): 31.

114 **"chinampas provided most of the food for the dense human population"** Perfecto, Vandermeer, and Wright, *Nature's Matrix*, 110.

114 **"produced one hundred million pounds of corn"** Peña, *Mexican Americans and the Environment*, 54.

114 **"most of the vegetables for the one million people then living in Mexico City"** Perfecto, Vandermeer, and Wright, *Nature's Matrix*, 110.

114 **"one of the most intensive and productive production systems ever developed"** Ebel, "Chinampas," 13.

114 **"created microenvironments that protected crops from frost"** Ebel, "China-mpas," 13.

114 **"hosted fungi that prevented the spread of pathogens"** Ebel, "China-mpas," 16.

114 **"sequestered significant quantities of carbon"** Ebel, "China-mpas," 14.

114 **"recent calls to revive the chinampas"** Renard et al., "Ecological Engineers Ahead of Their Time."

114 **"[locking] away large quantities of carbon"** Renard et al., "Ecological Engineers Ahead of Their Time," 39.

114 **"distinguished between soils with different textures and levels of fertility"** Peña, *Mexican Americans and the Environment*, 52.

114 **"the Mexica recognized some sixty different soil classes"** Peña, *Mexican Americans and the Environment*, 54; Devon G. Peña, "Sodbusters and the 'Native Gaze': Soil Governmentality and Indigenous Knowledge," in *Mexican-Origin Foods, Foodways, and Social Movements: Decolonial Perspectives*, ed. Devon G. Peña, Luz Calvo, Pancho McFarland, and Gabriel R. Valle (Fayetteville: University of Arkansas Press, 2017), 350.

115 **"a general term for soil that was appropriate for cultivation"** Devon G. Peña, "On Intimacy with Soils," in *Indigenous Food Sovereignty in the United States: Restoring Cultural Knowledge, Protecting Environments, and Regaining Health*, ed. Devon A. Mihesuah and Elizabeth Hoover (Norman: University of Oklahoma Press, 2019), 284.

115 **"a term for soil that had been degraded by careless farming practices"** Peña, *Mexican Americans and the Environment*, 54.

115 **"recognized soils as living organisms and felt an obligation to care for them"** Peña, "Sodbusters and the 'Native Gaze,'" 354.

115 **"devastating impacts on traditional farming systems in Mexico"** Gliessman, "Agroecology: Roots of Resistance," 27.

115 **"sought work as farm laborers in the United States"** Minkoff-Zern, *New American Farmer*, 40–45.

115 **"formally ended the ejido system of communal land tenure"** Minkoff-Zern, *New American Farmer*, 142.

115 **"Corn imports from the US spiked"** Minkoff-Zern, *New American Farmer*, 143–44.

115 **"Corn prices fell $160 per ton"** Minkoff-Zern, *New American Farmer*, 143–44.

115 **"as the number of Mexican corn producers fell by one-third"** Minkoff-Zern, *New American Farmer*, 143–44.

116 **"Some one million small farmers would be uprooted"** Devon G. Peña, Luz Calvo, Pancho McFarland, and Gabriel R. Valle, introduction to *Mexican-Origin Foods, Foodways, and Social Movements*, xviii.

116 **"In 2005, a researcher visited a rural village in southeastern Mexico"** Timothy A. Wise, "NAFTA's Assault on Mexico's Indigenous Farmers," Medium, March 25, 2020, https://medium.com/@tawise01/naftas-assault -on-mexico-s-Indigenous-farmers-d22be7b743b6.

116 **"the first effective oversight of pesticides"** Robert Gordon, "Poisons in the Fields: The United Farm Workers, Pesticides, and Environmental Politics," *Pacific Historical Review* 68, no. 1 (1999): 63.

117 **"managing their own farms"** Muna Danish, "More Latinx Farmers Own Their Land: Could They Make the Food System More Sustainable?" *Civil Eats*, April 15, 2019, https://civileats.com/2019/04/15/ag-census-more-latinx-farmers-own-their-land-could-they-make-the -food-system-more-sustainable/.

117 **"increased 21 percent between 2007 and 2012"** Danish, "More Latinx Farmers Own Their Land."

117 **"increased another 8 percent between 2012 and 2017"** United States Department of Agriculture National Agricultural Statistics Service, "Hispanic Producers," 2017 Census of Agriculture Highlights, 2019, https://www.nass.usda.gov/Publications/Highlights /2019/2017Census_Hispanic_Producers.pdf.

119 **"selecting away from plants that cooperate well with beneficial soil fungi"** Matthias C. Rillig, Carlos A. Aguilar-Trigueros, Tessa Camenzind, Timothy R. Cavagnaro, Florine Degrune, Pierre Hohmann, Daniel R. Lammel, et al., "Why Farmers Should Manage the Arbuscular Mycorrhizal Symbiosis," *New Phytologist* 222, no. 3 (2019).

120 **"Used as food, medicine, and even roofing material"** Miguel A. Altieri and Javier Trujillo, "The Agroecology of Corn Production in Tlaxcala, Mexico," *Human Ecology* 15 (1987): 201.

120 **"Agroecologist Helda Morales learned a memorable lesson"** John Vandermeer and Ivette Perfecto, "Complexity in Tradition and Science: Intersecting Theoretical Frameworks in Agroecological Research," chap. 6 in Méndez et al., *Agroecology*, 103.

121 **"has charted mind-bendingly complex pest control food webs"** Perfecto, Vandermeer, and Wright. *Nature's Matrix*, 179–80.

121 **"correlated the presence of these fungi with 'herbivore resistance'"** Guzman et al., "Crop Diversity Enriches Arbuscular Mycorrhizal Fungal Communities."

122 **"the desire to get away from pesticides is often the main reason"** Interview with Laura-Anne Minkoff-Zern, April 3, 2020.

124 **"more than 95 percent of the dominant tree species have utility"** Ronald Nigh and Stewart A. W. Diemont, "The Maya Milpa: Fire and the Legacy of Living Soil," in "Prescribed Burning," online special issue, *Frontiers in Ecology and the Environment* 11, no. s1 (2013): e46.

126 **"own just 3 percent of US farms"** Danish, "More Latinx Farmers Own Their Land."

126 **"never really came to agriculture"** Janine Jackson, "Our Food System Is Very Much Modeled on Plantation Economics," *FAIR*, May 13, 2020, https://fair.org/home/our-food-system-is-very-much-mod-eled-onplant ation-economics/.

126 **"agricultural ladder"** Minkoff-Zern, *New American Farmer*, 32.

127 **"became the new means for US agribusiness to exploit noncitizen workers"** Minkoff-Zern, *New American Farmer*, 36.

127 **"first recruited as temporary laborers during World War I"** Minkoff-Zern, *New American Farmer*, 40.

127 **"establishment of the Bracero Program"** Minkoff-Zern, *New American Farmer*, 40.

127 **"exploitative treatment and abuse"** Minkoff-Zern, *New American Farmer*, 41.

127 **"growers began encouraging others—without papers—to migrate"** Minkoff-Zern, *New American Farmer*, 41–42.

127 **"Termed "Operation Wetback," the initiative deported 1.3 million people"** Minkoff-Zern, *New American Farmer*, 42.

## Chapter 4. Putting Down Roots

133 **"These people, the Hmong, lived in remote mountain areas"** Jennifer Sowerwine, Nancy Peluso, and Christy Getz, "The Myth of the Protected Worker: Southeast Asian Micro-Farmers in California Agriculture," *Agriculture and Human Values* 32, no. 4 (2015): 584–85.

133 **"they began resettling in the United States"** Laura-Anne Minkoff-Zern, Nancy Peluso, Jennifer Sowerwine, and Christy Getz, "Race and Regulation: Asian Immigrants in California Agriculture," in *Cultivating Food Justice*, ed. Alison Hope Alkon and Julian Agyeman (Cambridge, MA: MIT Press, 2011), 80.

133 **"1,500 Southeast Asian farms in Fresno County"** Minkoff-Zern et al., "Race and Regulation," 75.

135 **"more than 50 percent of the vendors in some cities"** Jessica Jurcek, "Urge to Buy Local in Time of Pandemic Pushes Hmong Farmers to Move On-line," *Sahan Journal*, May 28, 2020, https://sahanjour nal.com/business -economy/urge-to-buy-local-in-time-of-pandemic -pushes-hmong-farmers -to-move-online/.

135 **"brought fresh vegetables back into communities"** Hmong American Farmers Association, "Our Story," https://www.hmongfarmers. com/story/.

135 **"rotational swidden agriculture"** Sowerwine, Peluso, and Getz, "The Myth of the Protected Worker," 584.

136 **"taking turns working one another's farms"** Sowerwine, Peluso, and Getz, "The Myth of the Protected Worker," 584.

136 **"had to be covered by workers' compensation insurance"** Minkoff-Zern et al., "Race and Regulation," 77–78.

136 **"defined as nuclear family members"** Sowerwine, Peluso, and Getz, "The Myth of the Protected Worker," 580.

136 **"multiagency labor law sweeps in Fresno County in 2004"** Minkoff-Zern et al., "Race and Regulation," 77–78.

136 **"seems disproportionately high"** Sowerwine, Peluso, and Getz, "The Myth of the Protected Worker," 580.

137 **"[Hmong] farms are typically so small . . ."** Minkoff-Zern et al., "Race and Regulation," 75.

137 **"at least fifty Hmong farms shut down"** Sowerwine, Peluso, and Getz, "The Myth of the Protected Worker," 580.

137 **"That wariness had far-reaching consequences"** Minkoff-Zern et al., "Race and Regulation," 79.

140 **"returned to their fields every form of waste . . ."** F. H. King, *Farmers of Forty Centuries* (N.p., 1911), quoted in Joji Muramoto, Kazumasa Hidaka, and Takuya Mineta, "Japan: Finding Opportunities in the Current Crisis," in *The Conversion to Sustainable Agriculture: Principles, Processes, and Practices*, ed. Stephen R. Gliessman and Martha Rosemeyer (Boca Raton, FL: CRC Press, 2010), 274–76.

141 **"These nations . . ."** King, *Farmers of Forty Centuries*, quoted in Muramoto, Hidaka, and Mineta, "Japan," 274–76.

141 **"a living mulch"** Muramoto, Hidaka, and Mineta, "Japan," 290.

141 **"earliest recorded use of cover crops"** Laura Paine and Helen Harrison, "The Historical Roots of Living Mulch and Related Practices," *HortTechnology* 3, no. 2 (1993): 137–43.

142 **"In the Lake Tai region, located in the Yangtze River Delta"** Stephen R. Gliessman, *Agroecology: The Ecology of Sustainable Food Systems*, 3rd ed. (Boca Raton, FL: CRC Press, 2015), 297.

142 **"Grain crops were rotated with legumes"** Luo Shiming, "Agroecology Development in China," in *Agroecology in China*, ed. Luo

Shiming and Stephen R. Gliessman (Boca Raton, FL: CRC Press), 19–20.

142 **"Mulberry leaves were used to feed silkworms"** Shiming, "Agroecology Development in China," 17.

142 **"Traditional agriculture in China . . ."** Shiming, "Agroecology Development in China," 17.

142 **"Chinese farmers started raising fish in rice fields"** Shiming, "Agroecology Development in China," 29.

142 **"Chinese farmers began raising ducks in their rice fields"** Shiming, "Agroecology Development in China," 29.

142 **"Closed-loop farming systems like those observed by King were commonplace"** Yadvinder Singh, C. S. Khind, and Bijay Singh, "Efficient Management of Leguminous Green Manures in Wetland Rice," *Advances in Agronomy* 45 (1991): 136.

143 **"I had learned how to grow healthy crops . . ."** Ivette Perfecto, John Vandermeer, and Angus Wright, *Nature's Matrix: Linking Agriculture, Biodiversity Conservation and Food Sovereignty*, 2nd ed. (New York: Routledge, 2019), 85–86.

143 **"particularly taken with the Indian farmers' system of composting"** Perfecto, Vandermeer, and Wright, *Nature's Matrix*, 85–86.

145 **"enough carbon to offset 8 percent of the direct annual greenhouse gas emissions"** Christopher Poeplau and Axel Don, "Carbon Sequestration in Agricultural Soils via Cultivation of Cover Crops—A Meta-Analysis," *Agriculture, Ecosystems & Environment* 200 (2015): 33–41.

146 **"seven out of eight farmworkers in the state were Chinese"** Minkoff-Zern et al., "Race and Regulation," 69.

146 **"the Chinese Exclusion Act of 1882"** Minkoff-Zern et al., "Race and Regulation," 69.

146 **"falsifying paperwork and exploiting loopholes in the law"** Minkoff-Zern et al., "Race and Regulation," 69.

146 **"two-thirds of Japanese Americans working in California were employed in agriculture"** Minkoff-Zern et al., "Race and Regulation," 70.

146 **"Japanese laborers used collective bargaining tactics to demand higher pay"** Minkoff-Zern et al., "Race and Regulation," 70.

147 **"about a third of all produce in California"** Minkoff-Zern et al., "Race and Regulation," 71.

147 **"a series of 'alien land laws'"** Minkoff-Zern et al., "Race and Regulation," 71.

147 **"largest Asian immigrant group legally ineligible for citizenship"** Minkoff-Zern et al., "Race and Regulation," 72.

147 **"bought land in the name of their US-born children"** Minkoff-Zern et al., "Race and Regulation," 72.

147 **"dummy corporations"** Minkoff-Zern et al., "Race and Regulation," 72.

147 **"designating Japanese farmers as employee 'managers' of land"** Minkoff-Zern et al., "Race and Regulation," 72.

148 **"acquire, possess, enjoy, use, cultivate, occupy, [or] transfer real property"** Minkoff-Zern et al., "Race and Regulation," 73.

148 **"a dozen states passed similar laws"** Minkoff-Zern, *New American Farmer*, 39.

148 **"the story repeated itself with one Asian immigrant community after another"** Sowerwine, Peluso, and Getz, "The Myth of the Protected Worker," 587.

148 **"to preserve the ideal of American homogeneity"** Minkoff-Zern, *New American Farmer*, 38.

150 **"the return on investment takes about seven years, minimum"** Rachael F. Long, Kelly Garbach, and Lora A. Morandin, "Hedgerow Benefits Align with Food Production and Sustainability Goals," *California Agriculture* 71, no. 3 (2017): 117–19, http://calag.ucanr.edu /archive/?article=ca.2017a0020.

150 **"driving a tractor by age ten"** David Mas Masumoto, *Harvest Son: Planting Roots in American Soil* (New York: W. W. Norton, 1998), 289.

151 **"invited to perform her one-woman show at the White House"** Monica Luhar, "Merging Farming and Art, Nikiko Masumoto Keeps Her Family's Roots Alive," NBC News, February 17, 2017, https:// www.nbcnews.com/news/asian-america/merging-farming-art-nikiko -masumoto-keeps-her -family-s-roots-n722471.

151 **"I came to realize one of the boldest, perhaps courageous things I could do . . ."** Luhar, "Merging Farming and Art."

151 **"The first Masumoto to immigrate to the United States"** Masumoto, *Harvest Son*, 13.

151 **"Her great-grandmother Tsuwa was next"** Masumoto, *Harvest Son*, 14.

151 **"The young couple logged long hours as farmworkers"** David Mas Masumoto, *Wisdom of the Last Farmer: Harvesting Legacies from the Land* (New York: Free Press, 2009), 4.

151 **"Raising five children on laborers' wages"** Masumoto, *Harvest Son*, 165.

151 **"some 120,000 Japanese Americans were sent to remote, makeshift prisons"** T. A. Frail, "The Injustice of Japanese-American Internment Camps Resonates Strongly to This Day," *Smithsonian*, January/February 2017, https://www.smithsonianmag.com/history /injustice-japanese-americans-internment-camps-resonates -strongly-180961422/.

151 **"Gila River War Relocation Center"** United States Department of the Interior, "Gila River Relocation Center," Japanese-American Internment Sites Preservation, January 2001, https://www.nps.gov/ parkhistory/online_books/internment/reporta7.htm.

151 **"they were again tasked with farm work—this time to feed themselves"** Masumoto, *Harvest Son*, 228.

152 **"better than doing nothing"** Masumoto, *Harvest Son*, 228.

152 **"died within a month of the family's arrival"** Masumoto, *Harvest Son*, 24.

152 **"falling in love with a restless young man from Block 23"** Masumoto, *Harvest Son*, 226.

152 **"Takashi Masumoto returned home to the Central Valley"** Masumoto, *Harvest Son*, 232; http://www.reedleyfuneralhome.com/obi tuary/6302551

152 **"Determined to better their circumstances"** Masumoto, *Harvest Son*, 229, 233.

153 **"scraped together enough money to purchase a cheap forty acres"** Masumoto, *Harvest Son*, 234.

153 **"My parents often used the Japanese term bachi . . ."** Masumoto, *Wisdom of the Last Farmer*, 31.

153 **"Taksahi's mom, Tsuwa, established a large garden"** Masumoto, *Harvest Son*, 287.

153 **"invented a new circuit technology"** Masumoto, *Wisdom of the Last Farmer*, 27.

153 **"Takashi and Carole began preparing for the day when they'd retire their tractors"** Masumoto, *Wisdom of the Last Farmer*, 27.

153 **"Mas decided to come home for a while"** Masumoto, *Harvest Son*, 119.

155 **"California farmers lost $1.7 billion"** Jay Lund, Josue Medellin-Azuara, John Durand, and Kathleen Stone, "Lessons from California's 2012–2016 Drought," *Journal of Water Resources Planning and Management* 144, no. 10 (2018).

155 **"Year 4 through 8 are peak production times . . ."** Liz Piña, "Lifespan of a Peach Tree," HMC Farms, March 21, 2019, https://www.hmcfarms.com/lifespan-of-a-peach-tree/.

156 **"approximately one-third of all food is wasted"** "Reduced Food Waste," Project Drawdown, https://drawdown.org/solutions/reduced-food-waste, excerpted from Paul Hawken, ed., *Drawdown: The Most Comprehensive Plan Ever Proposed to Reverse Global Warming* (New York: Penguin, 2017); Project Drawdown, *The Drawdown Review* (2020), 28.

156 **"twenty-eight times more potent than carbon dioxide"** Alejandra Borunda, "Methane, Explained," *National Geographic*, January 23, 2019, https://www.nationalgeographic.com/environment/article/methane.

156 **"could shave emissions by as much as ninety gigatons"** Project Drawdown, *Drawdown Review*, 26.

156 **"six times as much as we might save by switching to electric cars"** Project Drawdown, *Drawdown Review*, 39.

157 **"an overwhelming number of startups have developed apps and software"** Katerina Bozhinova, "16 Apps Helping Companies and Consumers Prevent Food Waste," GreenBiz, October 12, 2018, https://www.greenbiz.com/article/16-apps-helping-companies-and-consumers-prevent-food-waste.

157 **"inexpensive refrigeration 'bots'"** Aaron Munzer, "CoolBot Enables Small Farmers to Build Do-it-Yourself Coolers," Cornell Small Farms

Program, June 27, 2012, https://smallfarms.cornell.edu/2012/06/coolbot-enables-small-farmers-to-build-do-it-yourself-coolers/.

157 **"technologies that extend the shelf life of produce"** Andria Cheng, "Food Waste Startups Like FoodMaven Are Getting More Investor Attention Than Ever," *Forbes*, December 12, 2019, https://www.forbes.com/sites/andriacheng/2019/12/12/ugly-produce-no-more-food-waste-startups-are-hotter -than-ever/#4e4bf9e72ab2.

157 **"struggled to hold on to their flower farm"** Cathy Erway, "Bok Choy Isn't 'Exotic,'" *Eater*, April 8, 2019, https://www.eater.com /2019/4/8/18295351 /asian-vegetables-heirloom-farmers-farming.

158 **"reducing the flow some 20 to 30 percent"** Steve Holt, "How Buying Smaller Fruit Could Save California's Drought-Stricken Family Farms," KQED, June 29, 2015, https://www.kqed.org/bayareabites/97497/how-buying-smaller-fruit-could-save-californias-drought-stricken-family-farms.

158 **"their buyers said the apricot-sized peach was too small"** Sarah Fritsche, "How Masumoto Family Farm Is Trying to Sell Its Tiniest Peaches," *San Francisco Chronicle*, June 15, 2017, https://www.sfchronicle.com/food/article/Petite-peach-a-hard-sell-despite-enchanting-11214755.php.

158 **"Masumoto launched an #EatSmallFruit campaign"** Ezra David Romero, "Masumoto Family Farm Wants Americans To Value Petite Peaches," KVPR, June 27, 2017, https://www.kvpr.org/post/masumoto-family-farm-wants-americans-value-petite-peaches.

159 **"They wanted newly developed peach varieties"** Masumoto, *Harvest Son*, 129.

159 **"gave Mas and his peaches a shot"** Masumoto, *Wisdom of the Last Farmer*, 12.

159 **"helped Chez Panisse chef Alice Waters build a new culinary movement"** Nina F. Ichikawa, "Giving Credit Where It Is Due: Asian American Farmers and Retailers as Food System Pioneers," in *Eating Asian America: A Food Studies Reader*, ed. Robert Ji-Song Ku, Martin F. Manalansan, and Anita Mannur (New York: New York University Press, 2013), 278.

160 **"founded one of the country's first natural food markets"** Ichikawa, "Giving Credit Where It Is Due," 279.

## Conclusion

163  **"make up nearly 40 percent of the US population"** United States Census Bureau, "Quick Facts," https://www.census.gov/quickfacts /fact/table/US/PST045219.

163  **"more than 60 percent of the current population of agricultural laborers"** United States Department of Agriculture Economic Research Service, "Farm Labor," https://www.ers.usda.gov/topics/ farm-economy/farm-labor/#demographic.

163  **"food and sustenance Indigenous peoples provided to settlers"** Roxanne Dunbar-Ortiz, *An Indigenous Peoples' History of the United States* (Boston: Beacon Press, 2015).

163  **"own just 2 percent of the agricultural land in this country"** Jess Gilbert, Spencer D. Wood, and Gwen Sharp, "Who Owns the Land? Agricultural Land Ownership by Race/Ethnicity," *Rural America* 17, no. 4 (2002): 55–62, https://www.ers.usda.gov/webdocs/public ations/46984/19353_ra174h _1_.pdf?v=41056.

164  **"more than sixteen times smaller than the US agricultural land base"** Indian Land Tenure Foundation, "Land Tenure Issues," https:// iltf.org/land-issues/issues/; United States Department of Agriculture National Agricultural Statistics Service, "Farms and Land in Farms: 2018 Summary," April 2019, https://www.nass.usda.gov/Publications /Todays_Reports/reports/fnlo0419.pdf.

165  **"Canadian residential schools used brutal tactics"** Micah Luxen, "Survivors of Canada's 'Cultural Genocide' Still Healing," BBC, June 4, 2015, https://www.bbc.com/news/magazine-33001425.

168  **"98 percent of US farmland still in White hands"** Christopher Burns, Nigel Key, Sarah Tulman, Allison Borchers, and Jeremy Weber, *Farmland Values, Land Ownership, and Returns to Farmland, 2000–2016*, Economic Research Report No. 245 (Washington, DC: USDA, February 2018), https://www.ers.usda.gov/publications /pub-details/?pubid=87523.

170  **"some four hundred million acres"** Neil Thapar, "An Enormous Land Transition Is Underway: Here's How to Make it Just," *Civil Eats*, February 24, 2020, https://civileats.com/2020/02/24/an-enor mous-land-transition-is -underway-heres-how-to-make-it-just/.

170  **"25.1 million acres of US agricultural land"** Mitch Hunter, American Farmland Trust, personal communication, March 2, 2020.

170  **"generated seventy times as many greenhouse gas emissions"** Louise Jackson et al., "Adaptation Strategies for Agricultural Sustainability in Yolo County, California," California Energy Commission's Climate Change Center, July 2012 (CEC-500-2012-032).

171  **"now owns nearly two million acres of farmland"** Thapar, "Enormous Land Transition Is Underway."

175  **"farmers of color who helped design these policies"** Nadra Nittle, "Tracy McCurty Has Worked a Long Time to See Historic Wrongs Righted for Black Farmers," *Civil Eats*, March 29, 2021, https://civileats.com/2021/03/29/tracy-mccurty-has-worked-a-long-time-to-see-historic-wrongs -righted-for-black-farmers/.

# Index

# About the Author

Liz Carlisle is an assistant professor in the environmental studies program at UC Santa Barbara, where she teaches courses on food and farming. Born and raised in Montana, she got hooked on sustainable agriculture while working as an aide to organic farmer and US Senator Jon Tester, which led to a decade of research and writing collaborations with agroecological farmers in her home state. She is the author of *Lentil Underground* and coauthor, with Bob Quinn, of *Grain by Grain*, and she has written both popular and academic articles about food and farm policy, incentivizing soil health practices, and supporting new entry farmers. She holds a PhD in geography from UC Berkeley, and a BA in folklore and mythology from Harvard University. Prior to her career as a writer and academic, she spent several years touring rural America as a country singer.